THE REFERENCE SHELF VOLUME 37 NUMBER 4

REPRESENTATIVE AMERICAN SPEECHES: 1964-1965

EDITED BY LESTER THONSSEN

Professor of Speech
Metropolitan State College of Colorado at Denver

THE H. W. WILSON COMPANY
NEW YORK   1965

THE REFERENCE SHELF

The books in this series contain reprints of articles, excerpts from books, and addresses on current issues, social trends, and other aspects of American life, and occasional surveys of other countries. Six numbers, comprising a volume, are published in each calendar year. One number is a collection of recent speeches on a variety of topics; each of the others, devoted to a single subject, gives background information and discussion from various points of view and concludes with a comprehensive bibliography.

Subscribers to the current volume receive the books as issued. The subscription rate is $12 ($15 foreign) for a volume of six numbers. Single numbers are $3 each.

PREFACE

In 1963, more than 25,000 books were published in the United States. This does not include Government publications and brief pamphlets. As usual, fiction was the largest category. Writing in 1961, Paul Pickrel, long-time reviewer of books for *Harper's*, lamented the "appalling quantity" of novels and said "more of them achieve publication than the most partisan defender of fiction would regard as absolutely necessary for the survival of the art."

We can never learn accurately how many speeches are given in a single year. If we could, doubtless the detractors of rhetoric, not to mention those who are only mildly allergic to sustained talk, would conclude that destruction by words is imminent. Fortified by statistics, they would show that even the most patient listeners are nearing the limit of verbal endurance.

For many of us, however, the number of speeches often seems disappointingly small—of serious speeches, that is, which we can conveniently hear or read and which we believe worthy of preservation. This was true, oddly, in the year of a presidential campaign. Oratory was indeed a widely practiced art in 1964; but the quality of public utterance in political life was below reasonable expectations. Moreover, the "great debates" did not materialize, which compounded the disappointment. Believing that the 1960 experience had fixed television debates between presidential candidates as a permanent extension of the democratic process, the public understandably felt deprived of an opportunity to test the aspirants in the merciless trial of face-to-face competition.

Perhaps the most frequent criticism of the campaign was that the candidates did not discuss the issues. This is arguable, chiefly because an issue is hard to define. What for one person may seem to be a crucial matter may for another be an irrelevancy. I am reminded of a remark attributed to the late William J. Bulow, a

Democratic Governor and Senator from South Dakota. In a senatorial campaign against W. H. McMaster, the Republican incumbent, Bulow was asked what the issues were. His reply matched his reputation as a homespun humorist of the Will Rogers school: "There ain't any great issues, I guess. Mac's got the job and I want it." While the 1964 campaign cannot be described with such uncluttered simplicity, the conviction persists that urgent national and international questions did not get the kind of probing they deserved.

If political oratory in 1964 was disheartening, other types of speaking partially restored our faith. Particularly encouraging too was the continued—and it would seem heightened—interest of many quality journals in reprinting major addresses. We have long applauded the New York *Times* for making many important texts, either in full or in liberal part, available to its public. Good journals and magazines perform a like service, reprinting high-level addresses that would not ordinarily appear in full in the daily news media. I bring to mind C. P. Snow's "On Magnanimity" and Loren Eiseley's "The Uncompleted Man," both of which were printed recently in *Harper's*. On my desk before me are the Spring and Autumn copies of *American Scholar*. No fewer than five addresses are reprinted in the two issues: Paul B. Sears' "Telltale Dust," Jacques Barzun's "College to University—and After," Richard Hoggart's "Schools of English and Contemporary Society," James B. Conant's "Man Thinking about Man," and C. Vann Woodward's "The Question of Loyalty." Similar examples could easily be cited from other journals, notably *Atlantic, Science,* and *Saturday Review*.

I hope that this twenty-eighth issue of REPRESENTATIVE AMERICAN SPEECHES will contribute modestly toward keeping a selected group of addresses in public remembrance. I extend thanks to the contributors for permission to reprint their talks. I am also indebted to many colleagues and friends for help in the preparation of this volume, and especially to John Jamieson, Alexandra Hontchar, and Ruth Ulman of The H. W. Wilson Company, Mary Margaret Robb of the University of Colorado,

Laura Crowell of the University of Washington, Dorothea Thonssen, Ruth Taylor, Catherine Fatherson, Jacqueline Baxter Doolittle, Harry Doolittle, and Dr. E. S. Taylor of the University of Colorado Medical School at Denver.

LESTER THONSSEN

Alamosa, Colorado
August 1965

CONTENTS

SOME THOUGHTS ON MEN AND INSTITUTIONS

LONG STEPS ON A LONG TRAIL

AN ADDRESS TO A JOINT SESSION OF CONGRESS [1]

Lyndon B. Johnson [2]

"Voting as a badge of full citizenship has always had a special meaning to the Negro, but in 1965 the denial of the right cuts painfully and deeply into his new sense of personal dignity." So wrote Dr. Martin Luther King, Jr., during the tense days of the civil rights crisis in the early part of the year. He noted that at a time "when the Supreme Court has said that the law of the land demands 'one man, one vote,' so that all state legislatures may be democratically structured, it would be a mockery indeed if this were not followed without delay by an insistence upon 'one vote for every man.'"

On March 15, 1965, President Lyndon B. Johnson summoned a Joint Session of Congress and in a nation-wide radio-television address delivered what the New York *Times* called "the deepest commitment to the Negro cause of any American President." "Our mission," the President remarked, "is at once the oldest and the most basic of this country: to right wrong, to do justice, to serve man." And since many men and women are denied the ballot because of their color, "I will send to Congress a law designed to eliminate illegal barriers to the right to vote." After outlining the broad features of his recommendation, he appealed to all Americans to heed the call to duty, to conscience, to a high moral obligation:

> Above the pyramid on the great seal of the United States it says—in Latin—'God has favored our undertaking.'
> God will not favor everything that we do. It is rather our duty to divine His will. But I cannot help believing that He truly understands and that He really favors the undertaking that we begin here tonight.

The President's speech received strong praise and approval. Many regarded it as the most eloquent and significant of his Administration. Moreover, it demonstrated, as had his State of the Union address on January 4, 1965, that an important speech delivered during prime eve-

---

[1] Text furnished by George Reedy, press secretary to the President, with permission for this reprint.

[2] For biographical note, see Appendix.

ning time can be an effective instrument for widening political participation. Whereas Franklin D. Roosevelt had given one of his Messages over radio at an evening hour, Mr. Johnson was the first to use television. The President is not fond of the conventional press conferences. Accordingly, he has hit upon the device, seemingly effective, of presenting major statements to Congress and to the public simultaneously, and at an hour that will give him the largest possible audience. This would appear to be an adroit use of the mass communications media for taking his requests to the people.

David Brinkley wrote recently that "any man, President or not, turns in hour of need to the methods he uses with most facility." Since the President knows "he has no hope of winning his way with eloquence," continued Mr. Brinkley, he will rely on the methods he has used successfully: "the application of power heavily disguised as persuasion, and applied only when the outriders have reported in that the time is ripe." Conceivably the public may yet decide, however, that the President's capacity for eloquence is greater than the pundits believe.

I speak tonight for the dignity of man and the destiny of democracy.

I urge every member of both parties, Americans of all religions and of all colors, from every section of this country, to join me in that cause.

At times history and fate meet at a single time in a single place to shape a turning point in man's unending search for freedom. So it was at Lexington and Concord. So it was a century ago at Appomattox. So it was last week in Selma, Alabama.

There, long-suffering men and women peacefully protested the denial of their rights as Americans. Many were brutally assaulted. One good man, a man of God, was killed.

There is no cause for pride in what has happened in Selma. There is no cause for self-satisfaction in the long denial of equal rights of millions of Americans.

But there is cause for hope and for faith in our democracy in what is happening here tonight.

For the cries of pain and the hymns and protests of oppressed people, have summoned into convocation all the majesty of this great government of the greatest nation on earth.

Our mission is at once the oldest and the most basic of this country: to right wrong, to do justice, to serve man.

In our time we have come to live with the moments of great crisis. Our lives have been marked with debate about great issues, issues of war and peace, issues of prosperity and depression. But rarely in any time does an issue lay bare the secret heart of America itself. Rarely are we met with a challenge, not to our growth or abundance, or our welfare or our security, but rather to the values and the purposes and the meaning of our beloved nation.

The issue of equal rights for American Negroes is such an issue. And should we defeat every enemy, and should we double our wealth and conquer the stars and still be unequal to this issue, then we will have failed as a people and as a nation.

For with a country as with a person, "What is a man profited, if he shall gain the whole world, and lose his own soul?"

There is no Negro problem. There is no Southern problem. There is no Northern problem. There is only an American problem. And we are met here tonight as Americans, not as Democrats or Republicans, we are met here as Americans to solve that problem.

This was the first nation in the history of the world to be founded with a purpose. The great phrases of that purpose still sound in every American heart, North and South: "All men are created equal"—"government by consent of the governed"—"give me liberty or give me death." Those are not just clever words. Those are not just empty theories. In their name Americans have fought and died for two centuries, and tonight around the world they stand there as guardians of our liberty, risking their lives.

Those words are a promise to every citizen that he shall share in the dignity of man. This dignity cannot be found in a man's possessions. It cannot be found in his power or in his position. It really rests on his right to be treated as a man equal in opportunity to all others. It says that he shall share in freedom, he shall choose his leaders, educate his children, provide for his family according to his ability and his merits as a human being.

To apply any other test—to deny a man his hopes because of his color or race, or his religion, or the place of his birth—is not only to do injustice, it is to deny America and to dishonor the dead who gave their lives for American freedom.

Our fathers believed that if this noble view of the rights of man was to flourish, it must be rooted in democracy. The most basic right of all was the right to choose your own leaders. The history of this country in large measure is the history of expansion of that right to all of our people.

Many of the issues of civil rights are very complex and most difficult. But about this there can and should be no argument. Every American citizen must have an equal right to vote. There is no reason which can excuse the denial of that right. There is no duty which weighs more heavily on us than the duty we have to ensure that right.

Yet the harsh fact is that in many places in this country men and women are kept from voting simply because they are Negroes.

Every device of which human ingenuity is capable has been used to deny this right. The Negro citizen may go to register only to be told that the day is wrong, or the hour is late, or the official in charge is absent. And if he persists and if he manages to present himself to the registrar, he may be disqualified because he did not spell out his middle name or because he abbreviated a word on the application. And if he manages to fill out an application he is given a test. The registrar is the sole judge of whether he passes this test. He may be asked to recite the entire constitution, or explain the most complex provisions of state laws. And even a college degree cannot be used to prove that he can read and write.

For the fact is that the only way to pass these barriers is to show a white skin.

Experience has clearly shown that the existing process of law cannot overcome systematic and ingenious discrimination. No law that we now have on the books—and I have helped to put three of them there—can ensure the right to vote when local officials are determined to deny it.

In such a case our duty must be clear to all of us. The Constitution says that no person shall be kept from voting because of his race or his color. We have all sworn an oath before God to support and to defend that Constitution. We must now act in obedience to that oath.

Wednesday I will send to Congress a law designed to eliminate illegal barriers to the right to vote.

The broad principle of that bill will be in the hands of the Democratic and Republican leaders tomorrow. After they have reviewed it, it will come here formally as a bill. I am grateful for this opportunity to come here tonight at the invitation of the leadership to reason with my friends, to give them my views and to visit with my former colleagues.

I have had prepared a more comprehensive analysis of the legislation which I have intended to transmit to the clerks tomorrow but which I will submit to the clerks tonight but I want to really discuss with you now briefly the main proposals of this legislation.

This bill will strike down restrictions to voting in all elections—Federal, state, and local—which have been used to deny Negroes the right to vote.

This bill will establish a simple, uniform standard which cannot be used however ingenious the effort to flout our Constitution.

It will provide for citizens to be registered by officials of the United States Government if the state officials refuse to register them.

It will eliminate tedious, unnecessary lawsuits which delay the right to vote.

Finally, this legislation will ensure that properly registered individuals are not prohibited from voting.

I will welcome the suggestions from all of the members of Congress. I have no doubt that I will get some on ways and means to strengthen this law and to make it effective. But experience has plainly shown that this is the only path to carry out the command of the Constitution.

To those who seek to avoid action by their national government in their own communities, who want to and who seek to maintain purely local control over elections, the answer is simple.

Open your polling places to all your people.

Allow men and women to register and vote whatever the color of their skin.

Extend the rights of citizenship to every citizen of this land.

There is no constitutional issue here. The command of the Constitution is plain.

There is no moral issue. It is wrong to deny any of your fellow Americans the right to vote in this country.

There is no issue of states rights or national rights. There is only the struggle for human rights.

I have not the slightest doubt what will be your answer.

But the last time a President sent a civil rights bill to the Congress it contained a provision to protect voting rights in Federal elections. That civil rights bill was passed after eight long months of debate. And when that bill came to my desk from the Congress for my signature, the heart of the voting provision had been eliminated.

This time, on this issue, there must be no delay, or no hesitation or no compromise with our purpose.

We cannot, we must not refuse to protect the right of every American to vote in every election that he may desire to participate in. And we ought not, we must not wait another eight months before we get a bill. We have already waited a hundred years and more and the time for waiting is gone.

So I ask you to join me in working long hours, nights, and weekends if necessary, to pass this bill. And I don't make that request lightly. Far from the window where I sit with the problems of our country, I recognize that from outside this chamber is the outraged conscience of a nation, the grave concern of many nations and the harsh judgment of history on our acts.

But even if we pass this bill, the battle will not be over. What happened in Selma is part of a far larger movement which reaches into every section and state of America. It is the effort of American Negroes to secure for themselves the full blessings of American life.

Their cause must be our cause too. Because it is not just Negroes, but really it is all of us, who must overcome the crippling legacy of bigotry and injustice. And we shall overcome.

As a man whose roots go deeply into Southern soil I know how agonizing racial feelings are. I know how difficult it is to reshape the attitudes and the structure of our society.

But a century has passed, more than a hundred years, since the Negro was freed. And he is not fully free tonight.

It was more than a hundred years ago that Abraham Lincoln, the great President of the Northern party, signed the Emancipation Proclamation, but emancipation is a proclamation and not a fact.

A century has passed, more than a hundred years since equality was promised. And yet the Negro is not equal.

A century has passed since the day of promise. And the promise is unkept.

The time of justice has now come. I tell you that I believe sincerely that no force can hold it back. It is right in the eyes of man and God that it should come. And when it does, I think that day will brighten the lives of every American.

For Negroes are not the only victims. How many white children have gone uneducated, how many white families have lived in stark poverty, how many white lives have been scarred by fear because we wasted our energy and our substance to maintain the barriers of hatred and terror.

So I say to all of you here and to all in the nation tonight, that those who appeal to you to hold on to the past do so at the cost of denying you your future.

This great, rich, restless country can offer opportunity and education and hope to all—all black and white, all North and South, sharecropper, and city dweller. These are the enemies—

poverty, ignorance, disease. They are enemies, not our fellow man, not our neighbors, and these enemies too, poverty, disease and ignorance, we shall overcome.

Now let none of us in any section look with prideful right-eousness on the troubles in another section or the problems of our neighbors. There is really no part of America where the promise of equality has been fully kept. In Buffalo as well as in Birmingham, in Philadelphia as well as in Selma, Americans are struggling for the fruits of freedom.

This is one nation. What happens in Selma or in Cincinnati is a matter of legitimate concern to every American. But let each of us look within our own hearts and our own communities, and let each of us put our shoulder to the wheel to root out injustice wherever it exists.

As we meet here in this peaceful historic chamber tonight, men from the South, some of whom were at Iwo Jima, men from the North who have carried Old Glory to far corners of the world and brought it back without a stain on it, men from the East and West are all fighting together without regard to religion, or color, or region, in Vietnam, men from every region fought for us across the world twenty years ago. And now in these common dangers and these common sacrifices the South made its contribution of honor and gallantry no less than any other region of the great Republic. In some instances, a great many of them more. And I have not the slightest doubt that good men from everywhere in this country, from the Great Lakes to the Gulf of Mexico, from the Golden Gate to the harbors along the Atlantic, will rally now together in this cause to vindicate the freedom of all Americans. For all of us owe this duty; and I believe all of us will respond to it.

Your President makes that request of every American.

The real hero of this struggle is the American Negro. His actions and protests, his courage to risk safety and even to risk his life, have awakened the conscience of this nation. His demonstrations have been designed to call attention to injustice, designed to provoke change, designed to stir reform. He has called upon us to make good the promise of America. And who among us can say that we would have made the same progress were it not for his persistent bravery, and his faith in American democracy.

For at the real heart of battle for equality is a deep-seated belief in the democratic process. Equality depends not on the force of arms or tear gas but depends upon the force of moral right—not on recourse to violence but on respect for law and order.

There have been many pressures upon your President and there will be others as the days come and go, but I pledge you tonight that we intend to fight this battle where it should be fought, in the courts, and in the Congress, and in the hearts of men.

We must preserve the right of free speech and the right of free assembly. But the right of free speech does not carry with it as has been said, the right to holler fire in a crowded theater. We must preserve the right to free assembly but free assembly does not carry with it the right to block public thoroughfares to traffic.

We do have a right to protest, and a right to march under conditions that do not infringe the constitutional rights of our neighbors. I intend to protect all those rights as long as I am permitted to serve in this Office.

We will guard against violence, knowing it strikes from our hands the very weapons with which we seek progress—obedience to law, and belief in American values.

In Selma as elsewhere we seek and pray for peace. We seek order. We seek unity. But we will not accept the peace of stifled rights, or the order imposed by fear, or the unity that stifles protest. For peace cannot be purchased at the cost of liberty.

In Selma tonight—and we had a good day there—as in every city, we are working for just and peaceful settlement. We must all remember that after this speech I am making tonight, after the police and the FBI and the marshals have all gone, and after you have promptly passed this bill, the people of Selma and the other cities of the nation must still live and work together. And when the attention of the nation has gone elsewhere, they must try to heal the wounds and to build a new community. This cannot be easily done on a battleground of violence as the history of the South itself shows. It is in recognition of this that men of both races have shown such an outstandingly impressive responsibility in recent days, last Tuesday, again today.

The bill that I am presenting to you will be known as a civil rights bill. But, in a larger sense, most of the program I am recommending is a civil rights program. Its object is to open the city of hope to all people of all races, because all Americans just must have the right to vote. And we are going to give them that right.

All Americans must have the privileges of citizenship regardless of race. And they are going to have those privileges of citizenship regardless of race.

But I would like to caution you and remind you that to exercise these privileges takes much more than just legal right. It requires a trained mind and a healthy body. It requires a decent home, and the chance to find a job, and the opportunity to escape from the clutches of poverty.

Of course people cannot contribute to the nation if they are never taught to read or write, if their bodies are stunted from hunger, if their sickness goes untended, if their life is spent in hopeless poverty just drawing a welfare check.

So we want to open the gates to opportunity. But we are also going to give all our people, black and white, the help that they need to walk through those gates.

My first job after college was as a teacher in Cotulla, Texas, in a small Mexican-American school. Few of them could speak English and I couldn't speak much Spanish. My students were poor and they often came to class without breakfast, hungry, and they knew even in their youth that pain of prejudice. They never seemed to know why people disliked them. But they knew it was so. Because I saw it in their eyes. I often walked home late in the afternoon after the classes were finished, wishing there was more that I could do. But all I knew was to teach them the little that I knew, hoping that it might help them against the hardships that lay ahead.

Somehow you never forget what poverty and hatred can do when you see its scars on the hopeful face of a young child.

I never thought then in 1928 that I would be standing here in 1965. It never even occurred to me in my fondest dreams that I might have the chance to help the sons and daughters of those students and to help people like them all over this country. But now I do have that chance and I let you in on a secret, I mean to use it. And I hope that you will use it with me.

This is the richest and most powerful country which ever occupied this globe. The might of past empires is little compared to ours.

But I do not want to be the President who built empires, or sought grandeur, or extended dominion. I want to be the President who educated young children to the wonders of their world. I want to be the President who helped to feed the hungry and to prepare them to be taxpayers instead of taxeaters. I want to be the President who helped the poor to find their own way and who protected the right of every citizen to vote in every election. I want to be the President who helped to end hatred among his fellow men and who prompted love among the people of all races and all regions and all parties. I want to be the President who helped to end war among the brothers of this earth.

And so at the request of your beloved Speaker and Senator from Montana, the Majority Leader, the Senator from Illinois, the Minority Leader, Mr. McCulloch and other leaders of both parties, I came here tonight not as President Roosevelt came down one time in person to veto a bonus bill, not as President Truman came down one time to urge the passage of a railroad bill, but I came down here to ask you to share this task with me and to share it with the people that we both work for. I want this to be the Congress, Republicans and Democrats alike, which did all these things for all these people.

Beyond this great chamber, out yonder, the fifty states are the people we serve. Who can tell what deep and unspoken hopes are in their hearts tonight as they sit there and listen. We all can guess, from our own lives, how difficult they often find their own pursuit of happiness. How many problems each little family has. They look most of all to themselves for their futures. But I think that they also look to each of us.

Above the pyramid on the great seal of the United States it says—in Latin—"God has favored our undertaking."

God will not favor everything that we do. It is rather our duty to divine His will. But I cannot help believing that He truly understands and that He really favors the undertaking that we begin here tonight.

CIVIL RIGHTS AND FEDERAL RESPONSIBILITY [3]

WILLIAM L. TAYLOR [4]

On July 2, President Johnson signed the Civil Rights Act of 1964. It represented the end, though obviously not the complete solution, of a problem dating back a hundred years. Legislative maneuvering and debate on the bill lasted for a year. The House of Representatives considered the subject for some 74 hours; the Senate, for about 735 hours. The controversy filled more than 3,300 pages of the *Congressional Record*.

Among other things, the Act outlawed discrimination in public accommodations; permitted the stopping of appropriations to federally supported programs in which discrimination continued; and forbade discriminatory practices by both employers and unions. With the passage of the Voting Rights Bill, signed by President Johnson on August 6, 1965, two long steps in the drive toward fuller civil rights for all citizens were completed.

Reprinted below is a closely reasoned analysis of the issue of Federal responsibility and authority in dealing with acts of racial discrimination. The speaker was William L. Taylor, staff director designate and presently general counsel to the United States Commission on Civil Rights. In his address at a meeting of the Southern Political Science Association in Durham, North Carolina, on November 14, 1964, he examined two questions: What are the acts of racial discrimination for which remedies are sought? Who is engaging in the practices and is thus subject to restraint? After exploring the Federal-state relationship in this delicate issue, Mr. Taylor concluded:

Federal civil rights law is, after all, only a set of ground rules. The rules may avail us very little if action is not taken to establish the conditions of economic and social justice necessary to any meaningful exercise of rights. The rules can work properly only if strife is replaced by a spirit of cooperation and a determination to make progress. In short, every community and state in this nation is faced with the problem of working out a system under which all of its citizens can live together in harmony and in dignity. If those who believe in our Federal system are looking for a challenge, here it is.

[3] Text furnished by Mr. Taylor, with permission for this reprint.
[4] For biographical note, see Appendix.

We have become accustomed these days to saying, or at least hearing, that this nation is in the midst of a "revolution" in race relations. When we say this, we are recognizing that the protest against injustice to Negro citizens has grown more insistent, that many more people have become involved in the demand for a change, that the means for seeking redress have broadened to include direct and often dramatic nonviolent community action as well as more traditional appeals to the legal and political process, and that protest has, in some areas at least, resulted in significant change.

But if all of this constitutes a revolution, it is of a special sort —because the objective of the protesters is not to overthrow the national government or to restrain it from engaging in excesses in the use of authority. On the contrary, the most important goal of civil rights advocates is to compel the national government to exercise authority which it has not previously used or which it has not used effectively.

It is this demand for the exercise of national authority to prohibit acts of racial discrimination and to provide effective remedies for the denial of Federal rights which gives rise to legal and political controversy. For it is claimed by some that whether or not the conditions complained of are unjust, our system of constitutional government does not permit the national government to remedy them.

In examining this claim, a couple of preliminary observations about its changing character may be in order. During the past decade, the attack against the exercise of national authority has been leveled primarily against the Federal Judiciary, the branch of the government which was most active in declaring and vindicating the rights of Negro citizens. It was said not merely that Federal courts were interfering with the "rights" of states, but that they were usurping the prerogatives of the coordinate branches of the Federal Government by engaging in judicial legislation. With the passage of the Civil Rights Act of 1964, this issue has been rendered largely moot. Both Congress and the Executive Branch have now recognized and provided a means for implementing rights declared by the Judiciary. Thus, if a claim against national authority is to be successful in 1964, in most cases it must be sustained against the Federal Government as a whole, not simply against one of its coordinate branches.

It also seems to me that the attack upon the exercise of national authority does not rest as much today upon a moral defense of the existing order as it did some years ago. As the consequences of racial segregation and other forms of discrimination have become exposed to national scrutiny it has become much more difficult to defend such practices as being fair or just. The opponents of Federal action do not often say in candid conversation that the national government is attempting to deal with an imagined evil. Instead the argument is that the exercise of national authority is not an appropriate or effective way to deal with racial discrimination and that it may give rise to an evil greater than that which it seeks to correct.

But if this issue of Federal authority and responsibility is to be discussed in a meaningful way and not simply as an abstraction, we must talk specifically about the acts of racial discrimination for which a remedy is sought, and about who is engaging in these practices and may thus be subjected to restraint.

It has been clear since the end of the Civil War and the enactment of the Thirteenth, Fourteenth and Fifteenth Amendments that the national government has a responsibility to secure the rights of citizens to be free from discriminatory treatment at the hands of state and local governing authorities. Nowhere is this responsibility more explicit than in the matter of preventing racial disfranchisement. The Fifteenth Amendment specifically prohibits abridgment of the right to vote on account of race and vests in Congress the power to enforce its provisions. And there is very little argument that in a system of government which rests upon the consent of the governed the right to vote is fundamental to citizenship.

Thus, the effort of a few southern states over the past 75 years to keep Negro citizens from voting must rank as one of the most remarkable chapters in our nation's history of disrespect for law. From the grandfather clause to the white primary, as one device for disfranchising Negroes was struck down by the courts, other schemes replaced it. As a result, it has been estimated that there are still at least 100 counties in seven southern states where Negroes are systematically denied the right to vote.

Finally, in 1957 when it had become more than apparent that private remedies were insufficient, Congress authorized the Attorney General to sue in Federal court for injunctions against state registration officials who were disfranchising Negro citizens. But seven years later, despite the best efforts of the Department of Justice, Negro registration in the hard-core counties has risen from 5 per cent to only 8 per cent and Federal enforcement officials themselves admit that the law has been less than a resounding success.

The reasons for this are not hard to discern. The use of equitable remedies in the Federal courts is a traditional and often effective means of vindicating the rights of individuals, but it is not easily adapted to deal with mass deprivations of rights, especially when the offending parties have the power and resources for resistance that are available to state governments. The problem is aggravated by one of the informal checks of our Federal system—the veto power that U.S. Senators have over Federal judicial appointments in their states. The result of this practice has been the appointment of several Federal judges who have demonstrated through their conduct on the bench a notable lack of sympathy with the rights of the disfranchised and the requirements of Federal law.

Today, the chief instrument for disfranchisement is the misuse by local registrars of seemingly valid "literacy" or "educational" requirements to keep all Negroes—from the humblest sharecropper to the Harvard Ph.D.—from voting, while registering every white who can manage to print his name, and some who cannot. The defects of existing Federal remedies as means for eliminating such abuses of authority are not likely to be corrected by the Civil Rights Act of 1964. The new law continues to rely on the judicial approach to racial disfranchisement and merely seeks to ease the burden of proof upon the government and to speed the pace of litigation. Given the limitations of individual

lawsuits as a means for curing mass deprivations of rights and the
fact that the discretion of unsympathetic judges cannot easily be
restricted through legislation, application of the existing Federal
laws is not likely to result in any fundamental improvement of
the situation.

For these reasons, the Commission on Civil Rights and others
have suggested a radically different approach to the problem of
securing the right to vote—the appointment by the President of
locally based Federal officials to serve as temporary voting registrars and administer state registration requirements in a fair and
just manner.

There is no substantial doubt that a statute authorizing the
appointment of Federal registrars would be held to be an appropriate exercise of Congress' authority under the Fifteenth
Amendment and Article I, Section 4 of the Constitution. It is
true nonetheless that such a law would bring about a significant
alteration of Federal-state relations, and the decision to recommend this legislation was not one the Commission reached easily.
The dilemma is perhaps best reflected in the words of two
Commissioners—Dean Robert Storey of Texas and Dr. Robert
Rankin of North Carolina—who have always been greatly concerned about possible impingements of Federal authority upon the
prerogatives of states. Dean Storey and Dr. Rankin at first opposed the recommendation for Federal registrars upon these
grounds, and only later came to the reluctant conclusion that
such action was necessary:

> The evil of arbitrary disfranchisement has not diminished material-
> ly. The responsibility which must march hand-in-hand with states'
> rights no less than with civil rights has, as to the right to vote, often
> been ignored. Progress toward achieving voting rights is virtually at a
> standstill in many localities. For these reasons we have concluded sadly,
> but with firm conviction, that without drastic change in the means used
> to secure suffrage for many of our citizens, disfranchisement will con-
> tinue to be handed down from father to son. . . .
> Finally, we must state that survival of the honorable doctrine of
> states' rights imposes coterminous obligations. It is shortsighted indeed
> to force citizens of the state to look to the central government alone
> for vindication of rights about which there is no substantial disagree-

ment. As we have said on so many occasions: Civil rights carry with them civil responsibilities. So, too, states' rights carry with them state obligations to all its citizens.

The point is simply this: the right to vote is a cardinal principle of our constitutional system of self-government. The national government has been given plenary authority to take whatever steps are necessary to secure the franchise to all citizens without discrimination. Those who truly believe in our Federal system have hoped that it would be possible to achieve this without any basic alteration in the traditional relationships between the national government and the states. But they recognize that when this proves impossible, the states must yield. And, if the national government takes action which alters the familiar pattern of Federal-state relations, the responsibility, I submit, rests squarely with those who while proclaiming their devotion to our Federal system have, by refusing to recognize the rights of citizens, undermined it.

These observations are also pertinent to the problem of enforced racial segregation in public schools and other public facilities. When the Supreme Court outlawed the segregation of children in public schools, the decision undeniably came as a jolt to many, for it attacked a political and social system of great importance to a large part of the South. But it is wrong to suggest that *Brown v. Board of Education* represented a radical departure from established principles of constitutional government or a drastic alteration in Federal-state relations. During the sixty-year period in which judicial challenges to segregation laws were rebuffed, the Supreme Court never once denied that it had a responsibility to assure that all persons shall stand equal before the law. From *Plessy* onward the Court affirmed its authority and duty to strike down state legislation which disadvantaged the Negro, and it was able to sustain segregation laws only by indulging in the enormous fiction that they were not so intended and did not have that result. By 1954 the myth that laws which excluded a whole race from communal life were "equal" could hardly be sustained, and the Court applied established principle to strike it down.

During the decade that has elapsed since the decision, southern state governments have several times gone to the brink of precipitating a drastic change in Federal-state relations. If violence had been countenanced as a sustained policy of defiance, the Federal Government would have been compelled to employ force on a continuing basis in order to defend the rule of law. If public education had been abandoned, the Federal Government would have had the difficult task of deciding whether, despite a tradition of state and local control, education was too important a function in our society to be left entirely to local option. Fortunately, the day of massive resistance appears to be over, but the threat to our Federal system has not entirely disappeared.

The continued threat lies in the fact that a decree of the Supreme Court is being flouted by literally thousands of local school authorities who have deprived all but a very small proportion of millions of Negro children of their right to be assigned to public schools without regard to race. In the 1964 Civil Rights Act, Congress has attempted to deal with this situation by applying the same traditional remedy it previously employed in voting. The law authorizes the Attorney General to assert the interest of the United States and to protect the constitutional rights of Negro citizens by initiating suits for injunctions in the Federal courts. In some respects the judicial approach is more promising in education than in voting. But it is subject to the same limitations that are inherent in any effort to use individual lawsuits as a means for remedying mass deprivations of rights. And if the new law is not met with a spirit of cooperation that leads to progress, the resisting states will be inviting more direct Federal interference with the administration of public education—interference which will be necessary to defend the rule of law.

A story less well known than racial practices in voting and education is the involvement of the Federal Government, through its grant-in-aid programs, as a silent partner in discrimination. In general, grants-in-aid may be viewed as a positive example of cooperation in a Federal system, for the national government assists states in meeting important public needs under rules and regulations which safeguard against any assumption of undue

Federal control. But this policy of Federal noninterference in the administration of grants has for years been misapplied to permit "neutrality" with respect to the racial practices of the states, communities and institutions which receive such assistance. The results of such a policy have hardly been neutral—for under it, the Federal Government has helped to perpetuate inequality in education, to build all-white suburban neighborhoods, to provide employment opportunity for whites only and generally to subsidize the discriminatory practices of local governments and institutions.

In recent years, the Executive Branch has begun to abandon this false neutrality and to adopt a new policy under which, as President Johnson has said, "all members of the public should be equally eligible for Federal benefits financed by the public." President Kennedy did a great deal more in this area, the most dramatic example being his Housing Executive Order that Federal assistance would go only to those members of the housing industry whose homes are made available to all persons without regard to race. In issuing such executive orders and regulations, President Kennedy acted in part upon the authority of the Executive Branch to establish reasonable conditions in government contracts, in part upon the implied, and sometimes expressed, intent of Congress that facilities provided with Federal funds be available to all persons, and in part upon his constitutional duty to take care that the laws be faithfully executed. The President was supported in his action by a growing body of case law which takes into account the increasing involvement of government in the activities and operations of major private institutions. As these relations have developed and become more complex, the judiciary has subjected to constant reexamination the concept of "state action" under the Fourteenth Amendment. This has been necessary to make sure that acts of discrimination which the government was prohibited from engaging in directly were not accomplished indirectly. Thus, the test now is whether "to some significant extent the state in any of its manifestations has been found to have become involved" in private conduct which abridges individual rights; and the Fourteenth Amendment may be applied where there is "state participation through any arrangement, management, funds or property." This principle has been applied in a variety of contexts, most recently by the Fourth Circuit Court of Appeals, to prohibit discrimination by private hospitals receiving Federal assistance under the Hill-Burton Act.

With the passage of the Civil Rights Act of 1964 all branches of the Federal Government have now participated in formulating national policy. Congress has declared that no person shall be denied the benefits of any program of federally financed assistance because of his race and has established an orderly procedure for assuring compliance.

The attacks upon this provision of the law have been characterized by a great deal of misrepresentation. The law does not regulate the conduct of individuals who are the ultimate beneficiaries of Federal assistance, but rather that of institutions and organizations which administer funds for the benefit of large segments of the public. One may quarrel with the decision of the national government to assist and subsidize particular areas of private enterprise. It is harder to argue that once such aid is accepted, government should not assume the responsibility for assuring that it will not be denied to some members of the public on the invidious grounds of race or color.

I have been dealing thus far not with Federal action designed to create new rights, but with measures to enforce a right which has been in existence for years—that of every individual to be free from discrimination at the hands of his government. In enacting the civil rights law, Congress has gone a step further and has established a new principle—that major nongovernmental institutions in our society cannot exclude people from participating in the life of the community because of their race. It has said that major businesses which serve the public cannot deny access to Negro citizens because of their race and that major employers and unions must provide employment opportunity based upon merit and not upon race.

Here the chief source of authority for the action of Congress is its power to regulate commerce among the states. The framers wrote the commerce clause during an era when there was not much commerce between the states and they probably could not have foreseen its importance to a society in which practically all business is done on a nationwide basis. But this was the genius of those who drew the Constitution, and as matters have turned out, one may observe with Dean Griswold that "these words (the commerce clause) have had more to do with making us a nation than any other provision of the Constitution. . . . Without the commerce clause, we should have had today what has been called the balkanization of the United States."

The establishment of a national standard of equal treatment in public accommodations and employment is a traditional application of the commerce power, not unlike many other regulations Congress has imposed upon the businessman in his dealings with customers and the public, as well as with his employees and other businessmen. Congress, in exercising the commerce power, has sought to protect the public from impure food, drugs and water, from unsafe appliances, from criminal and immoral acts, from price fixing and other restraints of trade. So we are not dealing with an exercise of authority which is unique or peculiar in its application. In fact, it is not even necessary to reason from analogy, because Congress in passing the aviation and interstate commerce acts, has acted directly under the commerce clause to prohibit certain acts of racial discrimination. And even in the absence of statute, the Supreme Court has held that racial discrimination constitutes a burden upon interstate commerce in violation of the Constitution.

It is not difficult to demonstrate that the persistence of racial practices in public accommodations and employment have had a harmful effect upon the nation—that our national economy is weaker than it should be because some citizens have not been given a fair chance to develop and use their skills, that racism has hampered the South in the development of an industrial economy, that racial exclusion has restrained travel and trade in the United States. But the evil of racial practices in business is even more fundamental. Negroes in many parts of the United States have been excluded almost entirely from participation as producers or consumers in the mainstream of community life. They have had to build their own minority society or have none at all. In a real sense we have indeed had a "balkanization" of the United States—along racial lines.

In the face of obvious injustice, much of the opposition to the public accommodations and fair employment legislation has been predicated on the ground that it constitutes a "dangerous precedent." But no one has said what it is a dangerous precedent for. The due process clause of the Constitution stands as a bulwark against laws which impinge upon the legitimate interests of businessmen. Are these legitimate interests violated by a law which merely prohibits a businessman who invites the public at large to trade with him from excluding a part of the public on the invidious ground of race? Precedent in the form of the traditional common law obligation of innkeepers and the decisions of state and Federal courts sustaining state fair employment and public accommodations laws against constitutional challenge tells us "no." Even in the absence of precedent, many of us would answer the question in the same way. It is difficult to see then how a law which subjects business to reasonable regulation for the purpose of enlarging the liberty of citizens can be construed as a precedent for potential unfair restraint of commercial activity.

Thus, it is fair to say that in recent years the national government has acted as a whole to restrain the use of power by government and institutions as a means for excluding millions of citizens from any meaningful participation in their society. The national government has acted, belatedly and reluctantly, because state and local authorities, far from exercising their own powers to protect the rights of citizens, have been the chief agents of discriminatory restraint.

Even if we had no constitutional history on the subject, we would be faced today with the necessity of making a national decision about racial discrimination. Our alternatives would be a nation based upon a caste system not unlike South Africa's, a nation in which there would be only one class of citizens who would stand equal before the law, or no nation at all, but only a loose confederation of states each free to deal with its citizens as it chooses. Is there any serious doubt about what our decision would be?

Fortunately, we do have a constitutional history relevant to our current dilemma. Expressed in the simplest terms, national action to secure civil rights is a practical application of Hamilton's declaration that "whatever practices may have a tendency to disturb the harmony between the states, are proper objects of Federal superintendence and control," and of Justice Marshall's dictum that we have "a Constitution intended to endure for ages to come, and, consequently, to be adapted to the various crises of human affairs." More specifically, the purpose of government action has been to effectuate the ideal of equal justice stated in the original Constitution and guaranteed in the post-Civil War amendments. If there is a more fundamental goal of democratic government, the opponents of civil rights law have not yet told us what it is.

Given the exercise of national authority to secure equal justice, what is left of our Federal system? A great deal, I submit. Those who talk glibly of "states' rights" often do not pay much attention to how our Federal system actually works. One would be hard put, for example, to overestimate the amount of time that the Federal Judiciary spends in according deference to state and local authority. Elaborate rules of comity have been promulgated to permit the broadest scope for working out solutions to judicial problems at the local level. Challenges to state laws must be heard by courts of three judges; they will require that state administrative proceedings be exhausted before any Federal judicial hearings; they will refer questions of interpretation of state law to the state courts; they will not reach the constitutional issue if the case can be settled without deciding it.

The principle of federalism reflected in these judicial rules has been under great stress in recent years, because states have used them as instruments for delay and evasion in civil rights cases. If the purpose of the rules continues to be subverted in this manner, there can be little doubt that they will be modified to assure that Federal courts can serve as forums for the prompt vindication of constitutional rights.

But further alterations of Federal-state relations are not inevitable. If states would concede the supremacy of Federal law, judicial rules of comity could be applied to serve their true purpose. Having accepted the necessity for according Negro citizens rights guaranteed to them under the Constitution, state and local authorities would in turn be accorded a great deal of freedom in deciding how these guarantees are to be implemented. These possibilities can also be seen in the homage that Congress has paid to federalist principles in the new civil rights law. In the public accommodations and fair employment sections of the Act, it has provided that states and localities which have their own antidiscrimination laws will have first crack at enforcement. Provisions such as these can be viewed cynically as "another attempt of the Federal Government to impose its will upon the states," or, more constructively, as a real opportunity to make progress in race relations without the necessity for further Federal intervention.

Federal civil rights law is, after all, only a set of ground rules. The rules may avail us very little if action is not taken to establish the conditions of economic and social justice necessary to any meaningful exercise of rights. The rules can work properly only if strife is replaced by a spirit of cooperation and a determination to make progress. In short, every community and state in this nation is faced with the problem of working out a system under which all of its citizens can live together in harmony and in dignity. If those who believe in our Federal system are looking for a challenge, here it is.

One final note; I have not mentioned what I believe to be the greatest threat to the survival of our Federal system—corruption of the law.

Ordinarily, there is nothing in our Federal system that is deemed to be more of a local responsibility than protection of the public safety. It is here that the most elaborate rules of Federal deference have been established; Federal courts will interfere with state criminal prosecutions only under the most extraordinary circumstances, and Federal law enforcement officials will rarely allow the exercise of their responsibilities to impinge upon those of state and local officers. But all of these rules are predicated upon an assumption that the legal systems of states and localities are fair and incorruptible and that only occasionally do serious errors arise which require Federal redress.

In some communities in this nation events have proved such an assumption to be critically wrong.

There are communities in the United States where Negro citizens live in terror of vigilante action, knowing that officers whose job it is to enforce the law will not protect them. There are communities in the United States where Negroes know that they cannot exercise their constitutionally guaranteed rights to assemble peaceably, to vote and to use public facilities and that if they try they will be arrested. There are communities in the United States where citizens are treated brutally by the police if they protest racial injustice. There are communities in the United States where judges abuse their offices by restraining lawful activity, requiring excessive bail and meting out harsh and discriminatory sentences, all in an effort to repress the exercise of rights.

The Federal Government has power to deal with such emergencies. If it were employed, it would mean the supplanting of local law enforcement officers with Federal officials authorized to use force to uphold the law. This would be a serious decision indeed and it is one which no Federal official wants either to make or to recommend. But if all of the current efforts to persuade and negotiate fail, the choice will lie between leaving American citizens utterly defenseless in the face of lawlessness or protecting them at the cost of a drastic change in the allocation of responsibilities among governments. Only the exercise of courage and wisdom by the leaders of state governments can save us from such a decision.

THE QUADRENNIAL MARATHON

CAMPAIGN SPEECH AT MADISON SQUARE GARDEN [1]

BARRY GOLDWATER [2]

During the week of July 13, 1964, San Francisco was host to 1,308 delegates to the Republican National Convention. The outcome of the meeting seemed fairly certain. Although Governor William Scranton of Pennsylvania had made hurried efforts during the past fortnight to generate momentum for his candidacy, the knowing observers saw little likelihood of his becoming a serious challenger to the front runner. They were right. In an atmosphere charged with the spirit of the old revival meetings, nearly 900 delegates gave their resounding endorsement to Senator Barry Goldwater of Arizona. By their action, moreover, they wrested control for the time from the predominantly eastern, liberal wing of the Republican party and gave the conservative group the long-sought opportunity to present its philosophy directly to the people for decision.

In his speech accepting the nomination, Mr. Goldwater touched upon the themes which later became the points of attack in the campaign: the threats to freedom posed by the "bully of communism"; the decay of moral standards; the continual erosion of private freedom through encroachment by the central government; and the need for improving our posture in national defense. The speech also contained a sentence which subsequently provoked bitter—and unresolved—debate over meaning and implication: "I would remind you that extremism in the defense of liberty is no vice." Mr. Goldwater closed his acceptance statement by affirming that the "Republican cause is not to level out the world or make its people conform in computer-regimented sameness." Instead, it "is to free our people and light the way for liberty throughout the world."

In the ensuing campaign, Mr. Goldwater and his running-mate, Representative William E. Miller of New York, traveled some 100,000 miles and gave about 350 speeches. By any reasonable standard, this is a grueling assignment to impose upon our candidates. (The mileage-speech totals for the Democratic candidates were about the same as for

[1] Text furnished by the Republican National Committee, with permission for this reprint.

[2] For biographical note, see Appendix.

the Republicans.) Even the Republican National Committee chairman, Dean Burch, in retrospective reflections on the campaign, questioned the practical value of it all, saying that the candidates "end up largely talking to their friends in a race against exhaustion, mouthing dreary ghostwritten speeches which often miss the true issues and influence virtually no one—all at monumental expense."

On October 26, 1964—about a week before the election—Mr. Goldwater gave his climax address of the campaign. Before an audience of some 18,000—plus an estimated 5,000 who, unable to get seats, heard the address over loudspeakers set up outside Madison Square Garden— the Arizona Senator made his only campaign appearance in New York City. In a wide-ranging speech which delighted the partisan audience, he closed by evoking what Peter Kihss of the New York *Times* called a "specter of a Federal Government that would make all sorts of decisions." Said Mr. Goldwater:

If I said to you tonight that the Federal Government will tell you what business you can be in—what profits you can make— where you can be in business;

If I tell you that the Federal Government will make decisions about schools and whether or not your child can pray in them; or if your child will attend a particular school to satisfy a slide rule quota;

If I say to you that the Federal Government will make vital decisions about your children when they're young and your parents when they're old;

If I tell you that the Federal Government will tell you how much to pay those you hire and what to charge for the things you sell;

If I told you tonight that the Federal Government will deny you the other side of every right—such as the right not to associate, as well as the right to associate;

If I told you all those things, what country would you think I was talking about?

Well, I'm talking about America! Today!

With God's blessing, let's get it back!

Campaign speeches do not ordinarily abound in specifics. On matters of foreign policy, perhaps, this is both understandable and proper for as Walter Lippmann once remarked, "an essential rule of good diplomacy is to avoid spelling out everything before the negotiation starts." Still, the voter, intent upon making a responsible decision, expects and deserves at least a modicum of concrete information along with the generalizations. Both Senator Goldwater and the President relied heavily on generalities. Whether or not the challenger, or attacker, loses more than the incumbent in such a circumstance, is debatable. At any rate, some observers were surprised, as John D. Pomfret of the New York *Times* said, that Mr. Goldwater did not "put more flesh on the bones of his charges."

I can't help wondering, sometimes, if you've asked yourselves why my campaign is what it is.

I wonder, my fellow Americans, if you think I don't know what views would be most popular. Do you think I don't know what labor wants to hear, what management wants to hear, what housewives and diplomats and white collar workers want to hear?

Do you honestly think, after all these years in politics, that I don't know the easy ways to get votes? The promises to make? The subjects to talk about—and the ones to avoid?

Well, I do!

Let me tell you—it's impossible to live in Washington these days and not learn these things.

Well, then, you ask why don't I take the easy way?

There are a couple of reasons. First of all, if I just went around telling people what they wanted to hear, I'd sound like Lyndon Baines Johnson. And I still think the American people are entitled to a choice.

But more important, if I had to cater to every special interest in the country to get elected, I wouldn't want the job.

If you ever hear me quoted in this campaign, saying soothing and comforting words about how wonderful everything is in the world and how secure the peace is and how strongly and firmly we stand as the leaders of Freedom—look again because somebody is kidding you!

If you ever hear me quoted as wildly and irresponsibly promising that wages will go up and prices down, that taxes will go down and spending up, that more and more power in the Federal Government means more and more freedom for the people—look again because somebody is kidding you!

If you ever hear me quoted as promising to make you free by forcibly bussing your children from your chosen neighborhood

school to some other one just to meet an arbitrary racial quota
—look again because somebody is kidding you!

Now let's get down to some basics.

I want to see an American nation and people that are healthy,
sound, prosperous, free, secure, and progressive. I would hope
that the interim President feels the same way.

The difference between us is that I say these things are best
attained and furthered through the free enterprise and individual
liberty upon which this nation was founded—the free enterprise
and individual liberty that account for our growth to greatness.

I have a deep faith in the manhood of American men—and in
American women.

There was a time when references to the principles that guided
our founding fathers were considered the very essence of Ameri-
canism—when the style of freedom that Americans have fought
and died for was considered the hope of the world.

If this is no longer true, then perhaps it is time for government by decree. Perhaps it is time to mold public opinion rather
than ask for it. Perhaps it is time for the people to come strag-
gling back inside the protective walls and settle down to squab-
bling over their shares of the public dole. As long as they're fed
three times a day, they can always be reminded that they enjoy
"freedom" from hunger.

You know, once before a great and self-governing people gave
up their liberty—a liberty far less than ours. They put themselves in the hands of their leader, asking only to be fed and
entertained. They traded their votes for "bread and circuses."
They traded their Senate for an Emperor.

We call them Romans. They lost their nation when they
traded away their freedom.

Let me refresh your memory about freedom. For thirty years
your own government has been changing the meaning of the
word. They began by telling us it meant freedom from want and
fear. They have now begun to suggest that it means freedom
from poverty and unemployment. Soon, no doubt, it will mean
freedom from work, from responsibility—even from worry.

My friends, these are the rewards of freedom, not freedom itself. Never forget, there was only one freedom—only one freedom—on which this nation was founded. That was freedom from government—from too much, oppressive government.

Those now in power would like us to forget that the right guaranteed us all was not happiness, but the pursuit of happiness.

I ask you tonight, what is happening to us?

Sometimes I think we should pity them because I'm not sure they know what they're doing. But it is a fact that Lyndon Johnson and his curious crew seem to believe that progress in this country is best served simply and directly through the ever-expanding gift power of the everlastingly growing Federal Government.

One thing we all know—and I assure you I do: that's a much easier way to get votes than my way. It always has been. It's political Daddyism and it's as old as demagogues and despotism.

You want something for nothing? The Federal Government will give it ⸱ ⸱ vou.

You want to avoid responsibility for bringing up your children and educating them? The Federal Government will take over.

You want to duck the job of facing your local problems and solving them? The Federal Government will do it for you.

Never mind the fact that the power and the money to do these things has to be taken from you before the Federal Government car ⸱⸱ them for you. Every step in this direction is a loss of freedom for you!

Relax. Don't worry. The Federal Government will do for you all those things you find unpleasant to do for yourselves. And daily that government will grow more powerful. Daily it will enter new businesses and practices, new areas of private enterprise, where it has no place.

And daily its leaders will expand their power to buy your votes and elect their own successors. Yes, expand their power over you, the people, far beyond anything ever dreamed of by the framers of our Constitution. And daily freedom goes down the drain.

And always, they are driving and confusing you with the basic dishonesty that permeates so much political campaigning.

I speak of peace. Your interim President tells you I want to start a war—which is ridiculous, and you know it.

I speak of strengthening the Social Security system. Your interim President tells you I want to destroy it—which is ridiculous, and you know it.

I refer to the fundamental principles on which our great country was founded. My opposition tells you I am living in the past—which is ridiculous, and you know it.

When I demand a more discriminating and practical foreign aid policy, the word is that Barry Goldwater is an isolationist—which I'm not, and you know it. You know we need a more discriminating and practical foreign aid policy.

Well, my friends, a man—an intelligent man—can carry on this silly political double talk just so long. And it seems to me the voters can listen to just so much of it. And I think you're reaching the end of your rope.

I am determined to penetrate the smokescreen that's been placed between you and me the only way I know how—by continuing to stand straight and talk straight.

I do recognize that there is a natural, human wish in the hearts of some people to find relief from worry, from fear, from the responsibilities of being people.

It is this very wish that makes them surrender their initiative and their independence in return for empty promises.

Empty promises are cheap—and cheaper by the dozen.

I, for one, am an ordinary mortal who cannot bring himself to make these unkeepable promises. I believe that the things we must do can only be done by truly free people, governing themselves.

I want to see us do it that way. I'm not ready for the Federal Government to take over those things which we haven't yet done, or even tried. I am not yet prepared to say that our inner needs —the needs to be looked after and protected and shielded and mothered—are going to force us, as they have other peoples, to give to our central government in Washington the same kind of power from which we bravely revolted in the first place.

I believe in the great American Dream. I say we can be a people led but not driven—governed, but not ruled—organized, but not regimented—taxed, but not bled.

I believe we were right when we decided that freedom meant being free—and that freedom is an endowment—a gift from God —when we founded not a government, but a more perfect union.

I believe that the hope of the world rests not with the American Government—but with the American people.

And now, perhaps you'd like to have me do a little political forecasting for you. Everyone else has been doing it.

Let me begin by telling you about some of the votes I'm not going to get.

The Nazi and Fascist types—the bigots—are not going to vote for me because my grandfather was a Polish Jew. But do we want these votes?

The Communists and radical left-wingers are not going to vote for me because I don't believe we should let the Communists frighten us out of our freedom. But do we want these votes?

The lazy, dole-happy people who want to feed on the fruits of somebody else's labor won't vote for me. But do we want these votes?

The Socialist, ADA-type followers of Hubert Horatio Humphrey are not going to vote for me. The ones who don't care if the Social Security system goes bankrupt as long as it keeps making more and more unkeepable promises—the ones who are willing to believe that communism can be "accommodated." None of them will vote for me. But do we want these votes?

Now, may I tell you who, I believe, will vote for me?

People who take the trouble to reread, thoughtfully, the Declaration of Independence and the Constitution of the United States will vote for me. They're the people who realize that too much government, no matter how juicy the promises sound, is against their best interest.

People who have learned to be suspicious of never-ending promises of "something for nothing"—they will vote for me.

People who have the courage and the intelligence to listen to the truth, and think about it. People whose votes can't be bought. They'll vote for me.

People who are sick to death of politicians coming out in favor of happiness and declaring war on misery. People who are fed up with so-called leaders of government promising to legislate worry out of existence. People who will listen for a little while to such transparent, vote-grabbing demagoguery and say— "Baloney."

They'll vote for me.

But most of all, it will be the people who know that something must be done.

When our Central Intelligence Agency reports our international prestige is already below the peril point, something must be done. Johnson is stalling because elections are coming.

Consider that dragged-out disarmament conference, laboring under the grave danger of commitments without adequate safeguards of compliance. Something must be done.

Johnson has adjourned the conference until after the election.

Americans are dying in Vietnam. He sits tight and silent until after the election.

Critical questions face the General Assembly of the United Nations. Will Russia be made to pay her debts to the UN or will they be forgiven. Johnson has postponed the opening session until after the election.

Think of Bobby Baker, Matt McCloskey, Billie Sol Estes—the 150 quickie security clearances and other lax security practices disclosed by the Otepka Hearings. But Lyndon Johnson clamps on the lid until after the election.

The Defense Department, the State Department, the White House itself—they all might as well wear large signs saying "Closed Till after Election."

Not that they aren't busy. The Department of Defense has been busy announcing the success of some missile and radar projects begun under President Eisenhower's Administration. The State Department has been busy avoiding issues and postponing critical business. And the White House goes night and day, directing the strategy and making excuses—claiming credit for all that's good and pleading ignorance of all that's evil.

Our Government is in a state of moratorium until "after the election." And the office of President is being occupied, on a part-time basis, by the interim President, who's busy sweeping the business of his office under the rug with Bobby Baker, Billie Sol Estes, Matt McCloskey, and goodness knows what else, until after election.

What kind of a private club are these people running? Whose government is it anyway? I say it's yours, not theirs.

People who know that the White House goes begging for a full-time tenant, who know that it must be occupied by a President of the people, not by a wheeler-dealer—people who know that giveaway promises can't cover up a policy of drift, deception and defeat—these people are going to do something about it.

That means you.

One last question:

—If I said to you tonight that the Federal Government will tell you what business you can be in—what profits you can make —where you can be in business;

—If I tell you that the Federal Government will make decisions about schools and whether or not your child can pray in them; or if your child will attend a particular school to satisfy a slide rule quota;

—If I say to you that the Federal Government will make vital decisions about your children when they're young and your parents when they're old;

—If I tell you that the Federal Government will tell you how much to pay those you hire and what to charge for the things you sell;

—If I told you tonight that the Federal Government will deny you the other side of every right—such as the right not to associate, as well as the right to associate;

—If I told you all those things, what country would you think I was talking about?

Well, I'm talking about America! Today!

With God's blessing, let's get it back!

AN ADDRESS TO THE NATION [3]

Lyndon B. Johnson [4]

No one was surprised on August 27, 1964, when the Democratic National Convention, meeting at Convention Hall in Atlantic City, New Jersey, named Lyndon B. Johnson as its presidential standard-bearer. With Senator Hubert H. Humphrey of Minnesota as his running-mate, he immediately opened the campaign which was to result, on November 3, in a landslide victory for the Democratic party.

The campaign, though bitter, will not rank as one of the most exciting in American history. Nor will the oratory in all likelihood be rated with the best. Perhaps face-to-face confrontations of the candidates would have been helpful. But the television debates which wise observers predicted, in 1960, would become permanent features of the political process, failed to come off.

True to a tradition of long standing, both parties held their final rallies at Madison Square Garden in New York City. President Johnson used the occasion, on October 31, to fill in some features of his vision of tht Great Society:

> This nation, this people, this generation, has man's first opportunity to create the Great Society. It can be a society of success without squalor, beauty without barrenness, works of genius without the wretchedness of poverty! We can open the doors of learning, of fruitful labor and rewarding leisure—not just to the privileged few, but we can open them to everyone.

The 1964 rallies at the Garden took on an historic interest because they symbolized the end of an era. The Garden will be torn down and replaced by a unit atop the Pennsylvania Railroad Station. For the veteran politician James A. Farley, former Postmaster General and national chairman of the Democratic party, the final meeting for President Johnson had a special poignancy. Having attended the rallies in New York since the early nineteen hundreds, Mr. Farley has memories of the times when many speeches were featured at the meetings. In an interview with a New York *Times* reporter, he remarked that "nowadays there are more entertainers, more show business people on hand. I'

[3] Text furnished by George Reedy, press secretary to the President, with permission for this reprint.

[4] For biographical note, see Appendix.

suppose the party thinks that people might not show up unless they have entertainers." One gathers from the interview that Mr. Farley's fondest memory is of Franklin D. Roosevelt's campaign rally in 1932.

Although given at the height of the campaign, the speech reprinted below transcends the usual appeal for the voters' support. It was delivered over a nationwide radio-television hookup on October 18, 1964. Doubtless it contains political overtones. Understandably, the Republican National Committee heard it as something more than a national security address. Its appeal to the Federal Communications Commission, however, for the right to free time to answer the speech was rejected. But for students of public address, the President's report is of more than passing interest. Shrewdly timed, carefully worded, it stands largely as an informative statement reminiscent of Franklin D. Roosevelt's early fireside chats.

Within the space of a few days, three major developments had occurred: a change of leadership in the Soviet Union, the detonation of an atomic bomb by Communist China, and the victory of the Labour party in Great Britain. Unlike some events of prime importance, this cluster did not require an appeal to action, except through the conventional resolve to remain a strong power in a troubled world. But, as Max Frankel of the New York *Times* remarked, in the midst of momentous changes that the United States "did not bring about, the world's greatest power had better just stand there—and say something." This the President did with forthrightness and candor.

My fellow Americans: On Thursday of last week, from the Kremlin in Moscow, the Soviet government announced a change in its leadership. On Friday of last week, Communist China exploded a nuclear device on an isolated test site in Sinkiang. Both of these important events make it right that your President report to you as fully and as clearly and as promptly as he can. That is what I mean to do this evening.

Now, let me begin with events in Moscow. We do not know exactly what happened to Nikita Khrushchev last Thursday. We do know that he has been forced out of power by his former friends and colleagues. Five days ago he had only praise in Moscow. Today we learn only of his faults. Yet the men at the top today are the same men that he picked for leadership. These men carried on the administration of the Soviet government when he was absent from the Soviet capital, and that was nearly half of the time that he was in power.

Mr. Khrushchev was clearly the dominant figure in making Soviet policy. After Lenin and Stalin, he is only the third man in history to have made himself the undisputed master of Communist Russia. There were times when he was guilty of dangerous adventure. It required great American firmness and good sense—first in Berlin and later in the Cuban missile crisis—to turn back his threats and actions without war. Yet he learned from his mistakes and he was not blind to realities. In the last two years, his government had shown itself aware of the need for sanity in the nuclear age.

He joined in the nuclear test ban treaty. He joined in the hot line which can help prevent a war by accident. He agreed that space should be kept free of nuclear weapons. In these actions, he demonstrated good sense and sober judgment. We do not think it was these actions that led to his removal.

We cannot know for sure just what did lead to this secret decision. Our intelligence estimate is that Khrushchev learned of the decision only when for him it was too late.

There has been discontent and strain and failure—both within the Soviet Union and within the Communist bloc as a whole. All of this has been evident for all to see. These troubles are not the creation of one man. They will not end with his removal.

When Lenin died in 1924, Stalin took four years to consolidate his power. When Stalin died in 1953, it was not Mr. Khrushchev who first emerged. But two men now share top responsibility in the Soviet Union, and their exact relation to each other and their colleagues is not yet very clear. They are experienced, but younger men, and perhaps less rooted in the past. They are said to be realistic. We can hope that they will share with us our great objective—the prevention of nuclear war.

But what does all this mean for us in America? It means at least four things:

First: We must never forget that the men in the Kremlin remain dedicated, dangerous Communists. A time of trouble

among Communists requires steady vigilance among free men—
and most of all among Americans, for it is the strength of the
United States that holds the balance firm against danger.

Second: There will be turmoil in the Communist world. It is
likely that the men in the Kremlin will be concerned primarily
with problems of communism. This would not be all good, because there are problems and issues that need attention between
our world and theirs. But it is not all bad, because men who are
busy with internal problems may not be tempted to reckless external acts.

Third: This great change will not stop the forces in Eastern
Europe that are working for greater independence. Those forces
will continue to have our sympathy. We will not give up our
hope of building new bridges to these peoples.

Fourth: Our own course must continue to prove that we, on
our side, are ready to get on with the work of peace.

The new Soviet government has officially informed me,
through Ambassador Dobrynin, day before yesterday, that it
plans no change in basic foreign policy. I spoke frankly, as
always, to the Soviet Ambassador. I told him that the quest for
peace in America had never been more determined than it is
now. I told him that we intend to bury no one, and we do not
intend to be buried. I reminded the Ambassador of the danger
that we all faced two years ago in Cuba. I told him that any
Soviet government which is ready to work for peace will find us
ready in America. I said to the Ambassador that I would be ready
to talk to anyone, when it would help the cause of peace. I believe that this was a good beginning on both sides.

That same day, the Chinese nuclear device was exploded at
a test site near a lake called Lop Nor, in the Takla Makan
desert of the remote Central Asian province of Sinkiang. The
building of this test site had been known to our American intelligence for several years. In recent weeks the rapid pace of
work there gave us a quite clear signal that the long and bitter
efforts of this regime were leading at last to a nuclear test. At
first, in the 1950's, Russia helped the Chinese. This assistance

in the spread of nuclear weapons may now be regarded with some dismay in Moscow. We believe that this help was ended in 1960 as the quarrel among the Communists grew sharper. Soviet technicians left suddenly, with their blueprints under their arms, and the unfinished facilities were just left there standing, and the expected supplies were cut off. But the Red Chinese kept to their chosen purpose, even as their economic plans collapsed and the suffering of their people increased.

Our own distinguished Secretary of State, Mr. Rusk, gave timely warning as the preparations at Lop Nor advanced, and when the test occurred, I at once told the world that this explosion will not turn Americans and other free peoples from their steady purpose. No American should treat this matter lightly. Until this week, only four powers had entered the dangerous world of nuclear explosions. Whatever their differences, all four are sober and serious states, with long experience as major powers in the modern world.

Communist China has no such experience. Its nuclear pretensions are both expensive and cruel to its people. It fools no one when it offers to trade away its first small accumulation of nuclear power against the mighty arsenals of those who limit Communist Chinese ambitions. It shocks us by its readiness to pollute the atmosphere with fallout. But this explosion remains a fact, sad and serious. We must not, we have not, and we will not ignore it.

I discussed the limited meaning of this event in a statement on last Friday. The world already knows that we were not surprised; that our defense plans take full account of this development; that we affirm our defense commitments, in Asia; that it is a long, hard road from a first nuclear device to an effective weapons system; and that our strength is overwhelming now and will be kept that way.

But what I have in my mind tonight is a different part of the meaning of this explosion at Lop Nor. Communist China's expensive and demanding effort tempts other states to equal folly. Nuclear spread is dangerous to all mankind. What if there should come to be ten nuclear powers, or maybe twenty nuclear powers? What if we must learn to look everywhere for the restraint which our own example now sets for a few? Will the human race be safe in such a day?

The lesson of Lop Nor is that we are right to recognize the danger of nuclear spread; that we must continue to work against it, and we will.

First: We will continue to support the Limited Test Ban Treaty, which has made the air cleaner. We call on the world—especially Red China—to join the nations which have signed that treaty.

Second: We will continue to work for an ending of all nuclear tests of every kind, by solid and verified agreement.

Third: We continue to believe that the struggle against nuclear spread is as much in the Soviet interest as in our own. We will be ready to join with them and all the world in working to avoid it.

Fourth: The nations that do not seek national nuclear weapons can be sure that if they need our strong support against some threat of nuclear blackmail, then they will have it.

The two events I have discussed are large and full of meaning, and I will discuss them tomorrow with the legislative leaders. They are coming here to the White House for a full and complete briefing tomorrow afternoon. Yet they do not change our basic policy. We just reinforce it.

Now let me take a minute to say that the same thing is true about another important event this week. It is the victory of another party with another leader in Great Britain.

The British Labour Party is the same party that held power when the Atlantic Alliance was founded; when British and American pilots flew the Berlin Airlift together; when Englishmen joined us in Korea. It is a party of freedom, of democracy, and of good faith. Today it has the confidence of the British people. It also has ours. They are our friends—as the Conservatives before them are our friends—and as governments of both parties have been our friends for generations.

We congratulate the winners. We send warm regards to the losers. The friendship of our two nations goes on. This is our way with all our trusted allies.

This has been an eventful week in the affairs of the world. It is not the first such week, nor will it be the last, for the world has changed many times in the last twenty years. Great leaders have come and gone. Old enemies have become new friends. Danger has taken the place of danger.

Through this period we have steadily moved toward a more hopeful world. We have moved toward widening freedom and toward securing a more lasting peace. We will continue in this direction.

What happens in other countries is important. But the key to peace is to be found in the strength and the good sense of the United States of America. Tonight we are the strongest nation in all the world, and the world knows it. We love freedom and we will protect it and we will preserve it. Tonight, as always, America's purpose is peace for all men.

Almost eleven months ago, at a still more fateful hour, just after I had assumed the presidency, I spoke to all of the Congress and to our people of the purpose of America. Let me close tonight by repeating what I said then:

We must be ready to defend the national interest and to negotiate the common interest. This is the path that we shall continue to pursue. Those who test our courage will find it strong, and those who seek our friendship will find it honorable. We will demonstrate anew that the strong can be just in the use of strength; and the just can be strong in the defense of justice.

A HARD LOOK AT OUR FOREIGN POLICY

ETHICS IN INTERNATIONAL RELATIONS TODAY [1]

DEAN ACHESON [2]

"Nothing so fascinates and frustrates Americans as foreign affairs." So wrote Dean Acheson, Secretary of State from 1949 to 1953, in an article dealing with the impact of world opinion on our beliefs and actions. According to him, "world opinion is pure fancy"; it does not exist "on the matters which concern us." Why? "Not because people do not know the facts—facts are not necessary to form opinion—but because they do not know that the issues exist." At best, we can learn only what the government of a country or possibly the opposition likes to believe the people believe. Accordingly, world opinion "plays overtime upon our inferiority complexes."

> We are setups for the caricatures of the Ugly American, of the stupid diplomat, the contemptuous, grasping, wily foreigner taking our money at the other end of the rat hole down which we fatuously pour it, or our obtuseness in getting into wars we should have stayed out of, and getting out of wars we should have stayed in and enlarged.

He is sure that our image will "take care of itself if we get on with what we have to do. . . ."

Mr. Acheson has masterly talent for questioning cherished beliefs. A highly articulate, forthright man, he thrives on difficult assignments, and he has had many of them. Now a partner in a Washington, D.C., law firm, he continues to advise government officials and most recently represented President Johnson in mediation efforts in the Cyprus crisis.

In a speech at Amherst College, Amherst, Massachusetts, on December 9, 1964, he probed the old moralisms and maxims now used in making decisions on foreign policy. The "vocabulary of morals and ethics," he said, "is inadequate to discuss or test foreign policies of states." Instead of the moralistic we should use the strategic approach in our relations—"to consider various courses of action from the point of view of their bearing upon major objectives."

His thesis provoked extensive discussion. Some interpreted it as an abandonment of moral principles in our conduct toward other nations;

---

[1] Text furnished by Mr. Acheson, with permission for this reprint.

[2] For biographical note, see Appendix.

others regarded it as the defensibly realistic line that would safeguard our interests and ideals.

While Mr. Acheson made only incidental reference to Southeast Asia, he expressed an idea which might well serve as the backdrop against which to project the arguments developed in the three speeches following by Secretary of State Dean Rusk and Senators Wayne Morse and Gale McGee.

> Is it moral to deny ourselves the use of force in all circumstances, when our adversaries employ it, under handy excuses, whenever it seems useful to tip the scales of power against every value we think of as moral and as making life worth living? It seems to me not only a bad bargain, but a stupid one. I would almost say an immoral one. For the very conception of morality seems to me to involve a duty to preserve values outside the contour of our own skins, and at the expense of forgoing much that is desired and pleasant, including—it may be—our own fortunes and lives.

The discussion of ethics or morality in our relations with other states is a prolific cause of confusion. The righteous who seek to deduce foreign policy from ethical or moral principles are as misleading and misled as the modern Machiavellis who would conduct our foreign relations without regard to them.

Most of what we, and a good part of the non-Communist world, regard as ethical principles relates to conduct, the behavior of individuals toward one another. There is pretty general agreement that it is better to act straightforwardly, candidly, honorably, and courageously than duplicitously, conspiratorially, or treacherously. This is true of conduct toward friends and toward those who are ill-disposed to us. It is well that our Government should give to foreigners as well as to our own people as clear an idea as possible of its intentions. To do so should inspire confidence and increase stability. One need not counsel perfection—for instance, to tell the whole truth; but it ought not to be too much to advise telling nothing but the truth—advice which might usefully have been given to President Eisenhower before he began issuing statements about the U-2 aircraft shot down some years ago over the Soviet Union.

The French school of diplomacy, founded by Cardinal Riche-
lieu, the dominant school for nearly three centuries, and probably
still the best ever devised, was based, as François de Callières
stated, upon the principle that "open dealing is the basis of confidence" (a very different idea from President Wilson's ill-con-
sidered maxim, "open covenants openly arrived at"). He adds,
"The negotiator therefore must be a man of probity and one who
loves truth; otherwise he will fail to inspire confidence." And
again, "Deceit is the measure of the smallness of mind of him
who uses it . . . a lie always leaves behind it a drop of poison. . . .
Menaces always do harm to negotiation. . . ."

It does not detract from the purity of his morals that he sup-
ports them with worldly wisdom:

The diplomatist must be . . . a good listener, courteous, and agree-
able. He should not seek to gain a reputation as a wit, nor should he
be so disputatious as to divulge secret information in order to clinch an
argument. Above all the good negotiator must possess enough self control to resist the longing to speak before he has thought out what he
wants to say. . . . He should pay attention to women but never lose his
heart . . . , possess the patience of a watchmaker . . . should not be
given to drink . . . and be able to tell where, in any foreign country,
the real sovereignty lies. . . . Finally . . . a good cook is often an excellent conciliator.

For any of you who are contemplating a career in the Foreign
Service, François de Callières is as sound an adviser today as he
was in 1716.

Without laboring the point further, I take it as clear that,
where an important purpose of diplomacy is to further enduring
good relations between states, the methods—the modes of conduct—by which relations between states are carried on must be
designed to inspire trust and confidence. To achieve this result
the conduct of diplomacy should conform to the same moral and
ethical principles which inspire trust and confidence when followed by and between individuals.

The purpose of our own diplomacy, as of the French school,
requires the inspiring of trust and confidence, for our governmental goal for many years has been to preserve and foster an

environment in which free societies may exist and flourish. When we have said this, we had better stop and think before concluding that the policies which will advance us toward this goal can usefully be discussed or evaluated in terms of moral or ethical principles.

In the first place, a little reflection will convince us that the same conduct is not moral under all circumstances. Its moral propriety seems to depend, certainly in many cases, upon the relationship of those concerned with the conduct. For instance, parents have the moral right, indeed duty, to instill moral and religious ideas in their children and correct moral error. Ministers, priests, rabbis, and mullahs have much the same duties to their flocks, including that of correcting heresy, when they can make up their minds what it is.

But these same acts on the part of public officials—certainly in the United States—would be both wrong and a denial of the fundamental rights of the citizen. Indeed, even prayer prescribed and led by teachers in our public schools is condemned by our courts with the approval of some of our churches. The attempt of both governmental and religious bodies to censor literature, painting, sculpture, the theater, and the movies, under the aegis of those alliterative adjectives, lewd and lascivious, seems to me intolerable. Parents, if they are any good, can shield their children from whatever they choose. The rest of us had better take our chances with mortal sin, rather than to have policemen, trained to handle traffic and arrest ciminals, become judges of what art we may see or read. And it is just as bad when the local watch and ward society or church body tries to do the same thing.

So, acts, moral in one human relationship, may become quite the reverse in another. Generally speaking, morality often imposes upon those who exercise the powers of government standards of conduct quite different from what might seem right to them as private citizens. For instance, the moral, and indeed the legal, duty of a judge in bringing to bear upon a party before him the coercive power of the state is not to do "what he thinks is right," or by his decision to mould the kind of society which

seems to him to accord with divine will or high human aspiration. He has not been given this great power so that he might
administer personal justice, even though his conscience be as clear
as that of Harun al-Rashid or Henry the Second when they decided disputes by virtuous inspiration. Our courts are supposed
to be courts of law; and whatever justice may be (I know of no
satisfactory definition of it), it is to be achieved, as the phrase
goes, "under law." It is our hope that the consciences of our
judges will be guided, not by what they think is right, but what
they believe the law requires them to decide, whether they like
it or not.

So, too, what may be quite proper and moral for a private
citizen—for instance, the pursuit of personal advantage, or the
advantage of a group—often, and rightly, is condemned if done
when he assumes legislative or executive office. This distinction
is not always perceived and has gotten many people into trouble.
Even a candidate for office cannot expect the same latitude given
private individuals in exposing his ignorance and stupidity. November 3rd last made that rather clear.

Moreover, the vocabulary of morals and ethics is inadequate
to discuss or test foreign policies of states. We are told that what
is ethical is characterized by what is excellent in conduct and
that excellence may be judged by what is right and proper, as
against what is wrong, by existing standards. But when we look
for standards we find that none exist. What passes for ethical
standards for governmental policies in foreign affairs is a collection of moralisms, maxims, and slogans, which neither help
nor guide, but only confuse, decision on such complicated matters as the multilateral nuclear force, a common grain price in
Europe, policy in Southeast Asia, or exceptions and disparities
under the Kennedy Round of tariff negotiations.

One of the most often invoked and delusive of these maxims
is the so-called principle of self-determination. In the continuing dispute over Cyprus, it has been invoked by nearly all parties
to the struggle to support whatever they were temporarily seeking
to achieve—by all Cypriots to justify revolt against British rule,

by Archbishop Makarios to support an independent government
for the whole island, by Greek Cypriots as foundation for enosis
(union) with Greece, and by Turkish Cypriots for partition of
the island and double enosis, union of one part with Greece and
the other with Turkey.

Despite its approval by Woodrow Wilson, this maxim has a
doubtful moral history. He used it against our enemies in the
First World War to dismember the Austro-Hungarian and Otto-
man Empires with results which hardly inspire enthusiasm today. After the Second World War the doctrine was invoked
against our friends in the dissolution of their colonial connections. In all probability these connections would inevitably have
been dissolved. But the results were immeasurably improved
when considerations other than moralistic maxims were brought
to bear on the process.

On the one occasion when the right of self-determination—
then called secession—was invoked against our own Government
by the Confederate States of America, it was rejected with a good
deal of bloodshed and moral fervor. Probably you agree that it
was rightly rejected. You would doubtless also agree that the
dialogue now in progress between the British and French-speak-
ing sections of Canada upon the problems of a common national
life together would not be helped by conducting it in terms of
the principle of self-determination.

Furthermore, this moralistic doctrine is not merely no help
to wise policy decisions, it can be a positive menace to them.
"Hitler's appeal to national self-determination in the Sudeten
crisis in 1938," writes Henry Kissinger, "was an invocation of
'justice,' and thereby contributed to the indecisiveness of the resistance; it induced the Western powers to attempt to construct
a 'truly' legitimate order by satisfying Germany's 'just' claims.
Only after Hitler annexed Bohemia and Moravia was it clear
that he was aiming for dominion, not legitimacy; only then did
the contest become one of pure power."

Another set of moralisms and maxims crops up to bedevil
discussion and decision about what is broadly called "foreign

aid." A good deal of trouble comes from the anthropomorphic urge to regard nations as individuals and apply to our own national conduct vague maxims for individual conduct—for instance, the Golden Rule—even though in practice individuals rarely adopt it. The fact is that nations are not individuals; the cause and effect of their actions are wholly different; and what a government can and should do with the resources which it takes from its citizens must be governed by wholly different considerations from those which properly determine an individual's use of his own.

This does not mean that considerations of compassion have no place in governmental decisions. It does mean that the criteria are generally quite different and far more complicated. Some of these criteria will determine what funds can be made available; others will determine their allocation among uses always exceeding amounts available.

The overriding guide must be achievement of a major goal of policy—in this case, creating an environment in which free societies may flourish and undeveloped nations who want to work on their own development may find the means to do so. This is an exceedingly difficult matter for both aiding and aided governments. The criteria should be hard-headed in the extreme. Decisions are not helped by considering them in terms of sharing, brotherly love, the Golden Rule, or inducting our citizens into the Kingdom of Heaven.

But, you will say to me, at least one moral standard of right and wrong has been pretty well agreed to be applicable to foreign policy. Surely, the opinion of the world has condemned the use and threat of force by one state against another, as the United Nations Charter bears witness. Does this not give us firm ground on which to stand? Well, does it? Ever since the Charter was signed, those whose interests are opposed to ours have used force, or the threat of it, whenever it seemed to them advisable and safe—in Greece, Czechoslovakia, Palestine, Berlin, Korea, Indochina, and Hungary. Each side used it in regard to Suez.

Is it moral to deny ourselves the use of force in all circumstances, when our adversaries employ it, under handy excuses, whenever it seems useful to tip the scales of power against every value we think of as moral and as making life worth living? It seems to me not only a bad bargain, but a stupid one. I would almost say an immoral one. For the very conception of morality seems to me to involve a duty to preserve values outside the contour of our own skins, and at the expense of forgoing much that is desired and pleasant, including—it may be—our own fortunes and lives.

But, however that may be, those involved in the Cuban crisis of October 1962 will remember the irrelevance of the supposed moral considerations brought out in the discussions. Judgment centered about the appraisal of dangers and risks, the weighing of the need for decisive and effective action against considerations of prudence; the need to do enough, against the consequences of doing too much. Moral talk did not bear on the problem. Nor did it bear upon the decision of those called upon to advise the President in 1949 whether and with what degree of urgency to press the attempt to produce a thermonuclear weapon. A respected colleague advised me that it would be better that our whole nation and people should perish rather than be party to a course so evil as producing that weapon. I told him that on the Day of Judgment his view might be confirmed and that he was free to go forth and preach the necessity for salvation. It was not, however, a view which I could entertain as a public servant.

What, then, is the sound approach to questions of foreign policy? I suggest that it is what we might call the strategic approach—to consider various courses of action from the point of view of their bearing upon major objectives. On August 22, 1862, President Lincoln wrote to Horace Greeley in response to the latter's question as to how the President viewed the question of slavery in relation to the war then in progress:

My paramount object in this struggle is to save the Union, and is not either to save or destroy slavery. If I could save the Union without freeing any slave, I would do it; and if I could save it by freeing all the

slaves, I would do it; and if I could do it by freeing some and leaving others alone, I would also do that. What I do about slavery and the colored race, I do because I believe it helps to save this Union; and what I forbear, I forbear because I do not believe it would help to save the Union. I shall do less whenever I shall believe what I am doing hurts the cause, and I shall do more whenever I shall believe doing more will help the cause.

This is what I mean by the strategic approach. If you object that is no different from saying that the end justifies the means, I must answer that in foreign affairs only the end can justify the means; that this is not to say that the end justifies any means, or that some ends can justify anything. The shifting "combinazioni," sought by the weak Italian city states of the Renaissance to plunder one another, not only failed to justify the means they used, but gave their diplomacy and its expounder, Niccolò Machiavelli, the bad name they have today.

The end sought by our foreign policy, the purpose for which we carry on relations with foreign states, is, as I have said, to preserve and foster an environment in which free societies may exist and flourish. Our policies and actions must be tested by whether they contribute to or detract from achievement of this end. They need no other justification or moral or ethical embellishment. To oppose powerful and brutal states which threaten the independence of others is not less admirable because it helps secure our own as well; nor is it less good to help others improve their lot because it is necessary to keep the free world free and to strengthen it.

In conducting our foreign affairs we can use any amount of intelligence, perseverance, nerve, and luck. But if we have an excess of moral or ethical enthusiasm or idealism, let us not try to find an outlet for it in the formulation of foreign policies. Rather in how we carry them out. In this country we have an unfortunate tendency to do fine and noble things in a thoroughly churlish way. Let us remember that often what we do may be less important than how we do it. "What one lives for may be uncertain," writes Lord Robert Cecil; "how one lives is not." We can be faulted far less in what we do, than in how we do it.

TO WHAT PURPOSE WAR IN ASIA? [3]

WAYNE MORSE [4]

This was the year of the "-ins." There were sit-ins and lie-ins, chiefly in furtherance of the civil rights movement. A hospital "heal-in" made the news. Senator George A. Smathers of Florida suggested the need for a "think-in—a period of cooling-off by those pressing for expanded voting rights for all Americans." Columnist Art Buchwald talked about a "stand-in" that his children staged in the hall every night when they refused to go to bed. But perhaps the most dramatic innovation was the "teach-in," which attracted wide notice during the early part of 1965, and conceivably had some influence on the public policy of the United States Government.

Prompted by increasing criticism of our foreign policy, especially in Vietnam and Santo Domingo, students and faculty organized meetings at which lectures and debates on the wisdom and moral justifiability of our actions carried on over many hours, usually to large audiences, and invariably with great enthusiasm. The "teach-in" evidently originated at the University of Michigan with an all-night protest meeting on March 24, 1965. Immediately the idea spread to other campuses. By school's end, scores of meetings had been conducted at colleges and universities, large and small, across the land. While mildly critical of both the speeches and the "propagandistic" atmosphere at some of the protest meetings, Michael Levitas of the New York *Times Magazine* staff concluded that the "teach-ins" were "catalysts not only for the conversion of ideas, but for the dispersion of ideas. And when interest replaces apathy, the growth of a meaningful consensus will take care of itself."

Fully mindful of the possible impact of this movement on the public's attitude toward our foreign policy, the Government sent out what in effect were truth-squads to present, apparently without overwhelming success, the Administration's view of the puzzling crisis in Southeast Asia. Climaxing the academic dialogue was the so-called national teach-in at Washington, D.C., on May 15, where distinguished professors assessed the pros and cons of our policy. Before an audience of 5,000 and to an estimated 100,000 on some 100 campuses who heard the proceedings over radio, special telephone hookups, and television, the participants conducted what the New York *Times* called "the most com-

---

[3] Text furnished by Senator Morse, with permission for this reprint.

[4] For biographical note, see Appendix.

prehensive and civilized public debate on the Vietnamese war in all
the decade since the United States became involved in the conflict there."

One of the most outspoken and persistent critics of our actions in
Vietnam is Wayne Morse, senior Senator from Oregon and a member
of the Senate Committee on Foreign Relations. On April 23, 1965, at
the University of Oregon at Eugene, he took a major part in the meeting of the Faculty-Student Committee to Stop the War in Vietnam. A
former teacher of public speaking and argumentation at the University
of Minnesota, and a lifelong devotee and practitioner of debate, Senator
Morse believes deeply in the educative power of the spoken word. A
serious speaker little given to the use of humorous sallies and rhetorical
frills, he aims to present factual details that will assist the public in
arriving at responsible judgments. Consistent with this philosophy,
Senator Morse probed the question "Why are we fighting in Vietnam?"
and in his speech of April 23 concluded that

> The United States can accomplish nothing on the mainland of
> Asia so long as we are acting alone and in isolation from the large
> free nations of the area. To do so can mean nothing but per-
> petual war. Our present policy is not saving Asia from war or
> from communism, either, yet it compels our friends to choose be-
> tween one or the other. That is not an acceptable alternative to
> the people of Asia or of the United States, and I am satisfied that
> we have much more to offer by way of leadership if we apply
> President Johnson's admonition to "Come, and reason together."

It is with both pleasure and pride that I accepted your invitation to speak on behalf of the Faculty-Student Committee to
Stop the War in Vietnam. I am proud not only to be here, but
I am proud that the University of Oregon is part of a great
swelling tide of opposition in this country to the war in Asia, and
to the use of force which is rapidly becoming the monster that
controls its maker instead of the other way around.

There is today a war in Asia that is as much the making of
the United States as it is of any other country. And one cannot
read the daily paper or listen to the presentations of Administration officials in the confines of the Senate Foreign Relations
Committee without realizing that the only plans of the American
Government are plans for making it steadily bigger.

The whys and wherefores of this war are but vaguely known to the American people and even to the Congress. The contingencies being planned for are not known at all. The ways in which the bombing of the North are supposed to produce peace remain in the realm of pure mysticism.

Yet this week, Secretary of Defense McNamara, Ambassador Taylor, General Wheeler, General Westmoreland, Admiral Sharp, and other military commanders met in Hawaii to plan the further military steps by the United States within South Vietnam against North Vietnam. They take the form of the familiar prescription the military establishment has dished up for Southeast Asia for the last five years—to increase the South Vietnamese forces from 575,000 to 735,000 men, to build up American ground combat forces to several divisions, and to intensify the bombing of military targets and supply routes from the north into the south.

It is to the great peril of the United States and the American people that it is in a military conference of military men in Hawaii that the foreign policy of this country is being made, a foreign policy that is leading the American people into the jaws of both China and Russia, while at the same time stripping us of friends and allies in all parts of the world.

Five years ago we were concerned about a civil war in Vietnam. So we threw American money, weapons, and prestige into that war in an effort to turn the tide in favor of the faction we preferred. Today, more than 30,000 United States troops are in the war, hundreds of American aircraft are attacking North Vietnam, and more of the same is being planned. From a civil war in South Vietnam, the conflict has seen North Vietnam brought directly into the battle, the setting up of Soviet anti-aircraft missiles to ward off United States planes, and the preparation by China to send its armed forces into the fray.

All this has come about because the United States has preferred war to seeing itself proved wrong and mistaken in its support ten years ago of Ngo Dinh Diem.

The take-over by the military of American policy in Asia is producing not one advantage for the United States. It is not strengthening freedom in Vietnam, North or South. It is not gaining friends, admirers, or allies in Asia for the United States. Yet if it is not to strengthen freedom and maintain strong allies in Asia, what in the world is our policy in Asia?

Why are we fighting? Why do we insist that South Vietnam must remain non-Communist (one cannot say "free" because it is not free)? Why do our advocates of more war in Vietnam believe the United States must fight the Vietcong itself if it is not for the notion that by so doing we are going to establish and maintain some kind of anti-Communist ring around China and North Vietnam?

The whole object of the war effort is to contain China and to keep the other nations of Asia from falling into her sphere. But the use of military means to reach that end is destroying the very end itself.

It is destroying it by driving into opposition the countries we claim we are saving.

There are in Asia six nations that in terms of area, population, industrial capacity, and resources must be regarded as major powers. They are the Soviet Union, China, India, Pakistan, Japan, and Indonesia. Of these, we are driving headlong into direct military conflict with two: China and the Soviet Union. In fact, our expansion of the war by bombing North Vietnam made that result inevitable, for it compelled both those Communist countries to compete with each other in the race to come to the aid of North Vietnam.

So when the Soviet Union announced that many "volunteers" desired to go to North Vietnam, and offered its anti-aircraft missiles, with Russian technicians to man them, China upped the stakes by announcing its preparations to send the Chinese army into the fray, not as volunteers, but in defense of a country on its borders that was under attack.

Nearly all the assessments offered to date by our American spokesmen have sought to allay fears that the war in Vietnam would drive China and Russia back together. Time and again, questioning members of Congress have been told that such a result was not considered likely, because Russia is too anxious to concentrate her attention and resources on improving the living standards of her own people.

But what is at stake for Russia and China is the leadership of the Communist world. Neither can afford to allow a sister Communist state, especially a small one, to be shot up like a fish in a barrel by the United States without coming to her aid in one form or another.

It is not a question of whether China and Russia are going to become warm international bedfellows. But it is a question of whether they are going to put men and weapons into North Vietnam that will mean a major war with the United States, and that is exactly what both are preparing to do.

Where do we stand with the other great powers of Asia? How about Pakistan and India?

Because Pakistan has persistently criticized the United States war effort in Vietnam, and expressed a certain degree of sympathy and support for China in recent years, a planned visit to this country by its President Ayub was postponed at our request. And in order to even up things between Pakistan and her arch enemy, India, we asked Prime Minister Shastri to postpone his visit, too.

Mr. Shastri promptly announced he was canceling his visit to Washington, though he would come to Canada, and to Moscow. Next June we will witness the spectacle of a Prime Minister, on the receiving end of close to half a billion in American aid each year, visiting Canada, from where he receives next to nothing, but passing up the United States because our relations are too strained. That, incidentally, tells you a lot about our foreign-aid program, as well as our policy in Asia.

The reaction to Washington's postponement of the visits has not only been violent, but has served to strengthen both Pakistan and India in their objections to United States intervention in Asia. Mr. Shastri, for example, repeated his demand that the United States halt its air attacks on North Vietnam, a statement widely hailed in India as one that "stands up" to President Johnson and what Indian papers are calling his bullying diplomacy. For the first time in his career, Mr. Shastri has all political factions in India firmly united behind him in his response to the clumsy attempt to whip India into line along with Pakistan on the question of the war in Vietnam.

In Pakistan, we read that the toll of United States dead in Vietnam does not alter the image of the struggle there as one with racial overtones in which the United States is seen as insensitive to the military devastation of an Asian country. Memories of Hiroshima are being evoked, and the government-controlled Pakistani newspapers are pointedly asking whether the United States would be risking its present bombing strategy in any European country. A leading newspaper, *Dawn,* observes that it is "painful to see how little Americans know of the heart of Asia, where they want to act as perpetual policemen to 'protect' Asians against Asians. Should large-scale war flare up in Vietnam," it continues, "Asia will emerge in ruins and the very prospect which the West today dreads so much—the rise of communism—will then become a certainty."

A fifth leading nation of the area is Indonesia. In a recent television interview, President Sukarno responded to a question about Communist aggression in Vietnam with an insulting question of his own: "What Communist aggression?" On Wednesday we learn that Indonesia intends to be counted in on any Asian side against the United States, because that is the meaning of its announcement that thousands of "volunteers" are appearing at government offices to go to the defense of North Vietnam.

The only major Asian power that gives so much as lip service to the American war effort is Japan. Yet her people are so opposed to that war that the Japanese Prime Minister Sato sent his own personal representative to tour the area and to make his own assessment of the effectiveness and future of our policy. His report to Sato was all against us.

He found that probably 30 per cent of the Vietcong were Communists, that the Vietcong cannot be considered as controlled by either Hanoi or Peking, and that the United States was greatly mistaken in thinking that military force would solve matters. It may be some time before Japan officially changes its position but its repeated statements to China that Japan and China have no great conflicts between them is a hint of what is to come.

The war hawks and their newspaper mouthpieces will tell you that we must stop concerning ourselves with what other countries think, and do what *we* think is right in Asia. But everything they want us to do there is supposed to be for the benefit not of the United States, but of India, Pakistan, Japan, Indonesia, and the smaller countries of the area to save them from communism. Why is it, then, that they do not appreciate that we know better what is right for them than they do?

I suggest that the editorial I have quoted from *Dawn* tells our military leadership in the Pentagon something that they apparently will never figure out for themselves; namely, that the great advances made by communism have been made in the ruins of war. The destruction and desolation of military force can kill a lot of Communists. But it also makes Communists where none existed before. And it produces the disruption and breakdown of society which is the great opportunity that communism seizes.

There is nothing wrong with President Johnson's offer of April 7 to help develop the Mekong River Valley. But what is wrong with the speech he made on that occasion is that he revealed no plans for ending the war which is making development impossible anywhere in Southeast Asia. And within two weeks, his military high command was meeting in Hawaii to plan the next escalation of the action.

I ask you, as I have asked Administration officials as they have come before the Senate Foreign Relations Committee: Can you tell me how carrying the war to the north is going to bring an end to the war?

And the answer is the one we hear week after week from our Secretary of State, by way of his chant about making China and North Vietnam leave their neighbors alone. To go 8,000 miles away—alone—to make someone else leave their neighbors alone is perhaps the most hypocritical assumption of the role of international policeman that any nation ever claimed for itself.

It is not going to defeat the Vietcong. It is going to have no other result than to bring China and Russia, as well as the United States, into the war.

Why, indeed, should North Vietnam stop whatever it is that she is doing that Secretary Rusk cannot describe but what he assures us North Vietnam knows—when it has been our own position that we would not quit the war while we were losing? Do we think North Vietnam will cry "surrender" and ask for negotiations when we would not under the same circumstances? Do we think that North Vietnam will do as we say but not as we did, which was to escalate the war in order to put ourselves in a stronger bargaining position?

The returns are coming in on all these assumptions and they spell not peace on American terms but bigger and more terrible war.

I do not suggest that at any point has North Vietnam been innocent of illegal action under the Geneva Agreement. Nor do I doubt that in recent months and perhaps in recent years, the Vietcong movement has received considerable advice and support from North Vietnam. But violations by one side do not excuse violations by the other. Terrorist methods employed by one side have been matched by terrorism employed by the other. The United States had the clear duty and obligation under international law to petition the United Nations for redress of North Vietnam's violation of the Geneva Agreement. Why didn't we? History for generations to come will continue to ask the United States that question. It will also continue to find us as having been guilty of substituting the jungle law of military might for our often professed ideal of the rule of law through international agreement in cases of threats to the peace of the world. In Southeast Asia we have walked out on our ideals and joined the Communists in becoming a threat to the peace of the world.

Each escalation by the United States has resulted in a responding escalation within South Vietnam, and we are now at the point where the next escalation could well result in a direct response from Hanoi. Each violation and retaliation has served to worsen and not to improve the American position.

What I am saying is that our reliance upon wealth and military power to bring about a pro-Western government in South Vietnam has been a failure. It does not matter that our designs upon that country are not the same as were the French designs. Our methods are much the same, and they are failing every bit as surely as did the French methods.

If we do not seek traditional colonial objectives, we do seek in Vietnam the nationalist objective of American military security as we see it. We have already demonstrated that far from seeking the free political choice for the people of Vietnam we do not intend to let them choose anything contrary to American interests. We have let Vietnam and the entire world know that the United States considers South Vietnam as something to be "lost" or "held" by the United States, and we will kill as many of its people and destroy as much of its property as is necessary to "hold" it.

Our success with that objective is going to be all downhill, just as it has been downhill for ten years. We could not cope with rebellion within the south and now we cannot cope with assistance to it from the north. We have thrown our Seventh Fleet, hundreds of aircraft, and thousands of United States troops into the battle without success and we have not yet encountered the army of North Vietnam, much less that of China.

Our raids on North Vietnam have been illegal under the United Nations Charter. And they have failed in their purpose of making the Vietcong give up. One thing they *have* done has been to alienate the major countries of Asia and to cause serious alarm among the countries of Western Europe.

Our real problem in Vietnam is that we cannot control the situation by the means we know best—money and military force. We cannot control it because we want the area to remain pro-Western and to serve as a bulwark against Chinese expansion. Those are not realistic nor realizable objectives in the middle of the twentieth century. We never will have peace in Asia on those terms.

But we can have a peace in Asia when control of Indochina is removed from the ideological conflict between this country and China. To do that will require international supervision and self-determination for Vietnam. To return to the Geneva Accord offers some hope for ending the war. But it would require a return to the Accord by the United States and South Vietnam, too. In the end I expect that we will settle for just that, but in the meantime we and the world may pass through a trial of bloodshed before we find out that American fortunes in Asia are no more achievable than were French, British, and Dutch fortunes before us.

Neither the United States nor North Vietnam now has much chance to settle this terrible war by bilateral negotiations. It has gone too far. It is going much further if a third force consisting of the nations of the world who are not now involved in the fighting is not brought to bear on this Asian crisis. That is why many of us who are urging a negotiated settlement with honor and security for all participants have recommended a formal presentation of the threat to world peace created by the war to the procedures of the United Nations.

Unless the nonparticipating nations come forward and live up to their clear obligations under international law, they are not likely to be nonparticipants much longer. Mankind can very well be on the brink of a Third World War. Procedures of international law created by existing treaties do provide for the convening of an international peace conference on the crisis. I ask Great Britain, Canada, Japan, France, Russia, Italy, Belgium, Australia, New Zealand—yes, I ask all nations who profess that they want world peace—when, oh when, are you going to keep your obligations solemnly assumed by your signatures to existing treaties which provide for peaceful procedures for settling threats to peace? Is it your answer that they may not work? Then what is your alternative? War? The time has come for 85, 90, 95 and more nations to say to the United States and South Vietnam on the one hand and the Communist nations on the other who are jointly threatening the peace of the world: "We beg you to cease your fire and come to an International Conference Table."

Oh, I know the specter of Munich is immediately raised, and we are reminded that we could not do business with Hitler and it is better to fight now than later. But in all these comparisons with the years that led up to World War II, I never yet have heard anyone argue that the United States should, in 1938, have acted alone to send troops to Czechoslovakia to fight Germany. What the "Munich" criers have in mind for Munich is not that the negotiation should never have been held, but that a concert of nations should have acted together to serve notice and to take steps to stop further aggression. And that is what I am urging that we do in Vietnam.

The United States can accomplish nothing on the mainland of Asia so long as we are acting alone and in isolation from the large free nations of the area. To do so can mean nothing but perpetual war. Our present policy is not saving Asia from war or from communism, either, yet it compels our friends to choose between one or the other. That is not an acceptable alternative to the people of Asia or of the United States, and I am satisfied that we have much more to offer by way of leadership if we apply President Johnson's admonition to "Come, and reason together."

AN ACADEMIC LOOKS AT VIETNAM [5]

GALE McGEE [6]

Among the impressive speeches by the late President Kennedy was "The Education of an American Politician," delivered before the annual convention of the American Association of School Administrators and National School Board Association, at Atlantic City, New Jersey, on February 19, 1957. In it he remarked:

> There is considerable talk these days of the educational world's need for assistance from the political world. I am confident that assistance will be forthcoming. But I have also stressed to you tonight the assistance which the world of politics needs from the world of education; and to that end I ask your thoughtful attention to the task of uniting our two worlds still further.

Moreover, in his talk at Harvard University on June 14, 1956, he said "the political profession needs to have its temperature lowered in the cooling waters of the scholastic pool. We need both the technical judgment and the disinterested viewpoint of the scholar, to prevent us from becoming imprisoned by our own slogans."

Seemingly the academic world has responded to these appeals. As previously indicated, teach-ins, protests, and lively dialogues on foreign policy are everyday news. So much so that the Administration, though obviously favoring public discussion, has nonetheless found certain aspects of the intellectual ferment disturbing.

Currently there are several former professors in the United States Senate. Among them are Paul Douglas of Illinois, Eugene McCarthy of Minnesota, Karl Mundt of South Dakota, Wayne Morse of Oregon, Mike Mansfield of Montana, J. W. Fulbright of Arkansas, George McGovern of South Dakota, and Gale McGee of Wyoming. All of them have had a good deal to say about the problem in Southeast Asia. And in the wholesome spirit of dissent common to the academic community, they have differed widely in their views. Perhaps an interesting study could be made of the changes, if any, that took place in their thinking when they moved from the college or university hall to the Senate chamber. At least one of the Senators, Gale McGee, has commented on it. Writing in the *NEA Journal* of February 1963, he observed that two conclusions were quickly impressed upon him when he assumed senatorial responsibility:

---

[5] Text furnished by Senator McGee, with permission for this reprint.

[6] For biographical note, see Appendix.

First, the solutions to the world's problems, which seem relatively easy from an academic viewpoint, are not quite so simple from the viewpoint of someone in a position to affect policy. In the classroom, I had a lot more pat solutions to the problems of mankind than I now have in the United States Senate. As a teacher, I had often approached questions as either black or white, when in truth most are a shade of gray.

Secondly, I learned that I needed to revise my estimates on the art of politics and the responsibility of politicians. My intimate contacts with politicians, especially the 99 other Members of the Senate, have convinced me that they are a truly remarkable group, honestly dedicated to the public good.

In his speech to the United States Senate on March 29, 1965, Mr. McGee spoke both as a Senator and as a teacher. In the former capacity, he entered a defense of the Administration's policy in Southeast Asia; as a former professor of history at the University of Wyoming, he urged —as he had to groups of students and professors during previous weeks —against creating the impression that the campus debates were largely monologues rather than dialogues: "The image of the intellectual world is a one-sided image. It suggests that the students and their professors and intellectuals are all automatically pacifists or troublemakers, whose loyalty to their country may be open to question." He appealed to

the currently silent segment of our campuses who support the President or who may agree with fundamental tenets implicit in a firm posture in Asia to declare themselves now in a public way. Let the professors speak out; let the students petition. It is time to stand up and be counted.

Senator McGee closed his speech by saying that our responsibilities in Vietnam

are ugly and unpleasant, filled with suffering, death, and dislocation. But we have accepted them in the hope that in the final tally mankind will have benefited, that as a result of what we do here this year and next some peoples will have a chance to seek and find independence and self-determination that otherwise would have been denied them.

Active in debate and oratory while a student at Wayne (Nebraska) State Teachers College, and a teacher of the subject for several years, Senator McGee brings to his senatorial duties the talents of an accomplished and seasoned performer.

Mr. President, a great national debate on our policy in Vietnam has moved a considerable distance since it opened on the floor of the Senate on the seventeenth of February. It is with some reluctance that I take issue with my distinguished friend, the Senator from Alaska (Mr. Gruening), who has just preceded me, but he and I have had rather strong differences on this question for some time. Let me add that we have likewise enjoyed the additional pleasure of exchanging those differences, not only in debate on the floor of the Senate, but also in debate on some of the campuses of the universities across this great land of ours.

It is that kind of debate which, it seems to me, is in the tradition of free inquiry and open discussion in the test of conflicting positions in the public forum. This helps to firm up the wisdom of policy positions.

Because of the debates which have taken place in the past three months, we can now point to a higher level of both discussion and debate, but now more often on the right questions for the right reasons instead of the wrong reasons, and with not quite so much misinformation as characterized the opening discussions.

This is all to the good. The country as a whole has become much more closely attuned to the tough issues which need to be resolved in Southeast Asia. Much of the helpful delineation of the questions that plague our great country has come from high places in the Administration, led by the President himself, aided and abetted by Secretary of State Rusk and Secretary of Defense McNamara, as well as some of the President's closest personal advisers. Likewise, articulate voices in the Senate have continued to contribute to the discussion, and thus have contributed to the shaping of policy positions.

Not the least of the forces which have contributed to enlightened debate have been the voices that have come from the nongovernmental level, from town meetings, community seminars, and perhaps most of all from the campuses of our great educational institutions, both large and small.

The knowledge of the academic world in these matters has taken on new dimensions during this time of crisis. Perhaps more so than at any time since the 1930's, the college campuses have come forward to participate in a controversy with debate of high caliber and considerable magnitude.

As a former academic, I am delighted to see this manifestation of deep concern about an issue of such vital international and national significance.

Having said that, however, there is one aspect about it that remains disturbing to many of us. This is the seeming impression, which has come to us at least through the media of communication, that the campuses of the land are almost totally in the grasp of those who oppose the President's position in Vietnam, that they are engaging in a monologue rather than a dialogue. We are being led to believe that the teach-ins, the picketing activity, the marchings, and the public student demonstrations all reflect a cross-section of the campus life today.

It is unfortunate that this impression has gotten abroad in the land—unfortunate because it is not only unrealistic, but also because it is untrue. Yet at this very moment the image of the intellectual world is a one-sided image. It suggests that the students and their professors and intellectuals are all automatically pacifists or troublemakers, whose loyalty to their country may be open to question.

In the interest of objectivity, as we seek to judge the academic world of our time, particularly on the issue of Vietnam, it is necessary that we bear in mind how such distortion could emerge in the first place.

At the outset we ought to recognize that if the campuses were to rally around a policy that was already invoked, if the campuses were to accept what already is a fact, it would be less newsworthy and it would not attract attention from off the campus, and therefore the protester against the existing situation has the advantage in headlines.

Second, campuses generally and understandably draw hangers-on, those who are professional protesters, even though not officially members of the intellectual community. These hangers-on should not be confused with bona fide academics.

Third, major segments of the academic world have contributed through their intellectual resources to the warp and woof of the present American policy in Vietnam. The President himself is a former teacher. The Secretary of State was a professor of political science and a Rhodes scholar. The Secretary of Defense is a distinguished scholar Phi Beta Kappa. McGeorge Bundy, a key adviser to the President on defense matters, was dean of arts and science at Harvard. And Walt Rostow, chairman of the policy planning staff shaping these questions, was a professor of economic history at MIT and a Rhodes scholar.

In other ways, through position papers, field studies, public debates, and community dialogues, other voices from the classroom have helped to shape and to raise the level of understanding of the central issues in the Far East. On my own campus at the University of Wyoming my former colleagues in the department of history have taken the lead in this regard.

It is unfortunate in the light of this that only one side of the academic face is coming through—that which protests a strong policy in Indochina. One of the regrettable consequences is to give to the general public the wrong image of the intellectual in America—wrong only because it portrays him as being one sided and with a closed mind. It is not that students and professors should not protest, for whatever else, protest should ever remain a hallmark of academia. Exploration of the unrealistic as well as the realistic, of the frowzy as well as the fundamental, should always be a way of life on the campus. The right to think other-wise or be otherwise should remain a cherished tradition in the halls of ivy.

On a question of the magnitude of American policy in Viet-nam, it is important that the public image of the position of American intellectuals on it be brought back into balance. For all too long in our country's history academics were suspect, particularly in the public arena of politics. Among others, the Soviet Union frightened some of our countrymen into the realiza-tion that perhaps there was a proper place for intellect in a modern state. In any event, the intellectual has acquired a higher status and public respect today never before enjoyed—at least in this century. Thus, the campus is on the spot, and the urgency of getting through a balanced profile becomes even greater.

So I appeal to the currently silent segment of our campuses who support the President or who may agree with fundamental tenets implicit in a firm posture in Asia to declare themselves now in a public way. Let the professors speak out; let the students petition. It is time to stand up and be counted.

For several weeks, I have been meeting with groups of students and professors on the question of Vietnam. Their questions, their newspaper ads, and their picket signs generally center around half a dozen ideas. It has been my experience that the ideas often are noble but that the facts which led them to those ideas were often irrelevant. While ferment on the campus is to the good, we can ill afford campus monologues premised upon fermented facts, namely, facts that are old and out of date. How well I remember my own classroom days. It is with no thought of disparagement at all that I recall that Professor McGee had a lot more solutions to the problems of the world than does Senator McGee.

That may suggest, in capsule form, why President Truman, who may have held a different position until he became President, why President Eisenhower or President Johnson, too, came to about the same answers on this question. It is the difference between sheer speculation or posing theoretical postulates, and having to accept responsibility for taking a given policy position now on any given issue of the day.

Let us examine some of the questions and some of the answers to the questions which appear most frequently and most commonly in the student bodies with whom I have met, and many of the professors whom I know so well. These questions take into account the kinds of uncertainties that still prevail in many sincere and expert academic minds.

At the same time the answers take into account the radical changes in the status quo that have occurred in the last six to eight months.

Perhaps one question that is put most often, or most frequently, is this: Why do we interfere in what is largely a simple civil war between two factions in South Vietnam?

Of course, the answer to that question lies in the developments which have occurred in recent months. In that interval of time the government in Hanoi has intensified its training of skilled guerrilla forces, recruited in North Vietnam, and they have likewise stepped up their infiltration of the territory south of the seventeenth parallel.

Also, in recent months Hanoi has begun to give direct radio signals—orders, if you will—to most of the units operating in South Vietnam. This has meant coordination of movement and a concentration of targets, and thus a greater effectiveness or a greater threat of their capability to disrupt and destroy in the south.

Third, we now have abundant evidence to suggest that even major regular army units from Hanoi are now operating across the border in the south. There has begun wholesale importation of supplies and armaments from outside Vietnam, which are then smuggled into the south on behalf of the guerrillas. We have learned that in recent battles the Vietcong has been armed with small arms of which more than 90 per cent came from outside the area—notably arms from China, from Czechoslovakia. Almost 100 per cent of the larger weapons were of Chinese manufacture.

Until six months or so ago, the guerrilla operations were largely endemic in their nature. Very often they were cannibals from the standpoint of arms, either converting arms that they captured or using arms that they had discovered in caches left over from the Japanese occupation or the war with the French.

But that has now changed; and this change is the point to which we ought to lend emphasis as we seek to respond to the academics who still call into question policies in Vietnam on the basis of outmoded and outdated fact.

Another question that is commonly raised in the campus discussions is as follows: Why do we remain in a land that wants no part of our presence there, where a large segment of the population is openly trying to throw us out, and is strongly supporting the position of the guerrillas or the Vietcong?

That item, I submit, is nonsensical on its face. In the first place, how do we measure the attitudes of the rural peasant population in South Vietnam? How do we determine the state of mind of the people in the hills and the mountain country north of Saigon?

Mr. Gallup has not been over there. There is no known standard of measurement that would stand up to the test of validity. But one of the students suggested to me on one occasion: "Whenever the guerrillas come into a village, the first thing they do is to get cooperation from the local villagers."

Mr. President, students have often suggested to me that the best evidence of the fact that Americans are not wanted in Vietnam is disclosed in the fact that villagers themselves often aid the Vietcong by giving them rice, where possible, by helping them repair weapons, and even by supplying them with manpower. This cannot be denied as a fact, but in my judgment it is a fact that very often stems from terrorism of the most extreme sort. I suggest that most villagers, wherever the village, confronted by the shooting in cold blood of their tribal leaders or of decimation of their ranks by firing squads or by other atrocities practiced upon selected leaders of their community, would more readily surrender to a guerrilla occupation, however small, than try to resist them, only to suffer the same fate themselves.

The real point is that most of those people, being without adequate means to defend themselves, would find it easier to go along and cooperate, and perhaps spare the lives of the young ones or themselves, than to be mowed down by well-armed groups of terrorists from the ranks of the guerrillas.

On the other hand, terrorists have every advantage in some respects. In order to win, all that they have to do is to hit and run. All they have to do is to strike terror, not to deliver a program, and then fade away under cover of jungle or night, to strike again at some other place.

I reject, thus, the equation of the villagers cooperating with the terrorists with the opposition to the United States and our presence in Vietnam.

Another question that comes from the colleges suggests that, as a practical question, we are losing the war in Vietnam, anyway, and, therefore, we should not continue an effort to do better there; that we should get out while we can, and perhaps get out as gracefully as we can.

That point of view, too, is nonsense, as I see it. The war in Vietnam has been going on for ten years. At the very beginning it was said that the war could not last for more than six months. That kind of warfare has almost become a way of life because of practices and policies designed to unsettle and terrorize that have plagued the government in South Vietnam. This is not to make any apologies for the little game of "who is the president in South Vietnam" from time to time, for that in itself is another subject. But it is to say that the war is not lost and need not be lost in South Vietnam

A noted correspondent for the Paris weekly, *L'Express,* Georges Chaffard, has filed a series of dispatches which indicates that there has been a serious shifting, a significant one, in Vietnam. That statement comes from a source which, in general, has been sharply critical not only of the American position there, but of the Saigon government there as well. These articles report increasing cases of battle fatigue among the North Vietnamese and among guerrilla groups, whose ranks are no longer marching in a single step, as once was the case. It should be pointed out, as Joseph Alsop has mentioned in one of his columns, that Georges Chaffard is no friend of our present position there, but is merely recording a significant shift as he sees it on the spot. The correspondent does not predict, I hasten to add, an immediate end to the struggle. He has not pronounced that, therefore, in the wake of some depressing developments, there is suddenly to be a victory. What he is saying is that there has been a measurable shift, and it is the kind of shift that represents a basis for realistic judgment of the present policy that our Government has been pursuing in Vietnam.

Further, we now increasingly read in the press, reports of new cracks in the facade of intransigence, at Hanoi; cracks that suggest that the North Vietnamese themselves have become badly split due to the new pressures that have been imposed upon them.

Other correspondents write of vastly improved morale in South Vietnam, including the fact that 7,000 young men volunteered for military service in the South last month alone. A few months ago, the reports would likely have been that the same number of men had dodged the draft.

I would note that the picture is not all bright, and one would not find it wise to be overenthusiastic in the circumstances. There are those who still consider the conflict incapable of successful resolution, and they offer evidence to support their concept. But I insist that there has been a sufficient shift in the general complexion of affairs in South Vietnam today to sustain an attitude of guarded, cautious optimism, and a spirit of determination to continue the President's policy of a careful and planned use of force in North Vietnam.

We have also heard much of the idea that China represents the wave of the future in Southeast Asia, that its power will inevitably dominate the entire area. I would agree that China will certainly be of increasing influence in that area in future years, but that is a totally different concept than actual domination of smaller, weaker nations. On this point I subscribe to what President Johnson said at Johns Hopkins that "there is no end to that argument until all of the nations of Asia are swallowed up."

Some of the comment from those who protest our involvement in Vietnam casts us in the role of blood-thirsty warmongers, unmoved by the slaughter of innocents, the deaths of women and children, and completely unaware of the issues causing their deaths.

On Tuesday I had printed in the *Record* an editorial from the *Washington Post* entitled "Anguish of Power." That editorial pointed out that the responsibilities of world leadership, which cannot be ignored, present us with alternatives, all of which will result in bloodshed and human suffering. It noted:

Each of our decisions to use force or to fail to use force is filled with potential pain and injury for millions. This is the anguish that goes with great power. No one can deliver us from it.

The last question from the academic world which I will discuss here today—although there are many others—is the charge that we are all but alone in the nations of the free world in our policy in Vietnam, that we are earning universal condemnation and further tarnishing whatever good image is left us around the globe.

Let me say, that we must win our own respect first. We start with ourselves, to acquire what we regard as the best educated guesses, and we realize what our obligation is to mankind and to the world of which we are a part. We have to live with our conscience. We have to do what we believe in our best judgment is right because it is right, not because we are trying to win a popularity poll with some of the governments of the globe.

Any time we weigh foreign policy on the basis of taking a straw vote around the nations of the world, at that time we will be in deep trouble. This is not to suggest that we should ignore them. We must weigh and assess world opinion, national opinion, and the opinion of our colleagues, at all times. These are factors which we need to fit into the total scale of values which will guide us in our judgments. It does not mean that they should become a determining factor.

Those who are the most powerful in this world are rarely the most loved. Need I remind the Senate of the traditional role in history of the British nation for so many centuries, which in some respects became probably the most hated country in the world. We know that was true up and down the east coast of the United States for a long time. Especially was it true in Chicago during the 1920's, when the Mayor of Chicago ran his political campaigns based upon vilification of the King of England. This should remind us that with great power goes great responsibility and a great deal of unpopularity in the world.

We can never conduct our policies on the basis of trying to be loved by everyone or trying to be the good guy. We must do what the times require, for the simple reason that this is a world made up mostly of anarchy, and no one has agreed upon what rules we are to play as a result. There are others who are willing to be the bad guys, to take advantage of the inhibitions of civilization, of culture, of decent people, in order to exploit their inclinations not to act.

We dare not surrender to the temptation on the other side to exploit our respect for human life, our respect for the high level of civilization, and our abhorrence of war. One of the great calculations in the East has been the conviction that although the United States is a great power, that because of its highly civilized inhibitions it would not be willing to use its power. They are gambling on our unwillingness to use it.

It is not sufficient to suggest that because we have some new answers to old questions that we have sufficient justification for our role in Vietnam. We must ask ourselves—regardless of the success of our role—what business do we have in Vietnam at all. I submit that there are several reasons why to forfeit our presence in this troubled area would be to forfeit our leadership of the free world.

In the recent history of mankind the only force which has been able to keep international relationships on a peaceful plane has been that of balance of power. The Pax Britannica is a demonstration of how this concept, if pursued skillfully, can eliminate international conflicts on a global scale. And I would point out that though international conflicts once could be resolved upon the battlefields of Europe, this is no longer the case.

It makes a real difference to Southeast Asia where the line representing the balance of power is drawn. This line is fairly well determined across most of the globe but in Vietnam we have a soft spot that the Communists seek to exploit for the extension of their domination.

The nations of Southeast Asia have adopted the concept of wait and see over this struggle. For it is evident that the future course of these nations will be determined by our success or failure in stopping this pattern of conquest. Already we see the revival of Communist activity in Thailand, the Philippines, Indonesia, Laos, and Cambodia. The picture is clear: what can succeed in South Vietnam can succeed in these nations, too—and this applies for both sides in equal measure.

National independence is a concept for which peoples have died over the centuries. I am convinced that the independence of these nations from direct external control, no matter what is the nature or form of their government, best serves the interests of these nations and of world peace.

The policy of planned escalation of this conflict is the subject of the debate which began here in the Senate on February 17. That policy now is being carefully applied by the Johnson Administration. These are what I consider to be the goals of this policy:

First, we seek to set the stage for negotiations between the parties involved in this dispute. We mean to convince those who thought we were summer soldiers that we will honor our commitments in South Vietnam regardless of the discomfort, regardless of the size of the effort. I believe this fact is now becoming apparent to Hanoi and I believe the chances for meaningful negotiations are improving.

All of us readily admit, unless it be the most rabid militarist on the loose—and I trust there are none of those except in retirement—that there is no military solution to Southeast Asia. We will not solve the Southeast Asia problem with bullets, guns, and troops. We must reach the kind of stage at which it will be possible to sit down realistically and try to find some substitute for war there.

But in February we were in no position to negotiate. The other side was not disposed to negotiate. Why should they? They were convinced that they were going to get everything free. They would get all that they desired without sitting down with anyone. If they would only wait it out, the Americans would soon go home.

Thus, likewise, we had to acquire a position which would lead them to understand that we were there to stay, and that their only chance to realize some kind of settlement better than the drains on their resources that war was making is to talk.

So these, then, were the purposes of planned escalation.

Now, nearly three months later, it is possible to assess our Government's program with the advantage of hindsight. In spite of the attacks made by the critics of the President, in spite of the assaults on the part of those who thought that it would be suicide and that we ought to get out, it is now possible to note measurable progress through the policy of planned escalation.

Second, we seek to lessen the chances of accidental war. To those who believe that our policy is just the reverse, I would suggest that accidental wars are created by those who misread the intentions of their adversaries. A policy of uncertain response to aggression encourages that aggression and further aggression. At a certain point our alternatives would be exhausted and we would be at war. When the Communists understand our intentions, I believe the chances for accidental war will be materially lessened. We shall never be free of the threat of war, but we can reduce the risk as much as possible.

A third goal of this policy is the sealing off of the problem of South Vietnam. As George A. Carver, Jr., pointed out in an excellent article in the April issue of *Foreign Affairs,* there is a power struggle in South Vietnam, but neither of the two sides are connected with the Vietcong. The infiltration of men and arms from the North was stepped up in February in an attempt to solve all problems from the outside. The South Vietnamese should be given the chance to work out their own future and a closed border will help them do it. No one suggests that democracy as we know it can be installed there, but that is no reason to deny the South Vietnamese the right to plot their own future free from outside domination.

With these goals in mind, I firmly believe that we are making definite progress in this conflict. A cross-section of press accounts indicates the morale is increasing in the South. The increase in military volunteers has already been referred to. More and more weapons are being captured by the South Vietnamese Army. The ranks of the guerrilla forces are being thinned by the failure to replace casualties and the increasing number of deserters. More and more of these South Vietnamese trained in the North for guerrilla warfare return to their homes and families immediately upon being infiltrated southward. In many places they have shifted from offense to defense.

Further stresses and strains are visible in the Moscow-Peiping Axis. Name calling between the two is increasing and some physical conflict has appeared in Chinese student attacks upon Soviet Embassies and reversed incidents in Moscow.

In Hanoi there are increasing reports of a split in the ranks of policymakers. Young officers are contesting the strategy of the old revolutionaries. Doubts about the wisdom of present policies are increasing.

The announcement this morning that a battalion of Australian infantrymen are being sent to South Vietnam is welcome news which indicates that our allies have confidence in our ability to carry out our program and that we do not stand alone in this troublesome endeavor.

Finally, the President's speech in Baltimore, following as it did in the wake of American escalation and in the wake of a dispatch of increased troop personnel from the United States to Vietnam, came as a gesture of strength and of a sincere desire for peace, rather than being subject, instead, to being considered a desperate proposal by a nation that was on the ropes in Southeast Asia. That speech could not have been made in February with any dignity. That speech could not have received any kind of credence anywhere around the world two months before. But because of the acceleration that was planned in North Vietnam, it was possible to show to the rest of the world again the true face of America; namely, that we have no designs on anyone else's government, that we covet no other country's territory, and that our goal is peace wherever we can obtain it and in whatever proportions it can be achieved. We have shown to the world that we are willing to put our men, our money, our policy, and our hearts where our words have been. That is an important step forward.

None of these facts suggest that we shall be at the negotiating table next month, but they are signs that our policy is having the effect we wish it to have and that it should be continued.

The responsibilities we have accepted in Vietnam are ugly and unpleasant, filled with suffering, death, and dislocation. But we have accepted them in the hope that in the final tally mankind will have benefited, that as a result of what we do here this year and next some peoples will have a chance to seek and find independence and self-determination that otherwise would have been denied them.

Our policies, as a product of human endeavor, may not be perfect. They should be debated, discussed, analyzed, and criticized by those in our colleges and universities and by the man on the street. But it is my hope that these debates and discussions will be conducted with an objective view of the facts and in the context of honorable differences among honorable men. We have the choice of helping to steer the course of history or of muddying the waters with fruitless and irrational posturing.

AN ADDRESS BEFORE THE AMERICAN SOCIETY
OF INTERNATIONAL LAW [7]

DEAN RUSK [8]

On April 7, 1965, at Johns Hopkins University in Baltimore, President Johnson restated his "Pattern for Peace in Southeast Asia." In a widely discussed speech, he announced that "we will not be defeated. We will not grow tired. We will not withdraw, either openly or under the cloak of a meaningless agreement." He observed, however, that "we remain ready for unconditional discussion" and he announced his intention to ask Congress to join in a billion-dollar development program, hopefully with the cooperation of other industrialized countries, "to improve the life of man in that conflict-torn corner of our world." It was a firm speech—even a grim, tough, and crafty speech according to columnist Joseph Alsop—that redefined America's policy in Vietnam.

During the next two months the debate on this policy grew sharper. Periodic reaffirmation and defense of the official position became necessary. In an address dealing largely with "the lawful versus the unlawful use of force," Secretary of State Dean Rusk cited Vietnam as an instance in which our security—as well as our Allies'—"is threatened by those who would embark upon a course of aggression whose announced ultimate purpose is our own destruction." Speaking before the American Society of International Law in Washington, D.C., on April 23, 1965, Secretary Rusk said the lessons of the past thirty years show clearly "that the acceptance of aggression leads only to a sure catastrophe" and that aggressors "must face the consequences of [their actions] and be saved from the frightful miscalculation that brings all to ruin."

Students interested in making analyses of conflicting arguments on public issues should examine Secretary Rusk's address alongside Senator Morse's which appears on pages 62-72. Additionally, these speeches can profitably be compared with others by Senator Morse delivered at Johns Hopkins University on March 15 and at the Mock United Nations Assembly at Ohio University, Athens, on April 10; and by Senator Ernest Gruening of Alaska at the April 17 Rally of Vietnam sponsored by Students for a Democratic Society in Washington, D.C. These speeches, together with editorial comments and letters on the war in Southeast Asia, were reprinted in the *Congressional Record*, April 26, 1965, pages 8149-79.

[7] Text furnished by Pearl S. Knopping, Publications Distribution Officer, Office of Media Services, Department of State, with permission for this reprint.

[8] For biographical note, see Appendix.

When this distinguished Society was founded fifty-nine years ago, the then Secretary of State, Elihu Root, became its first president. With the passage of time, the secretary of state has been elevated to a less demanding role, that of honorary president. Secretary Root himself not only established the precedent of becoming president while Secretary of State; he also superseded it by continuing to serve as your president for eighteen years. The *Proceedings* of the first meeting indicate that Secretary Root not only presided and delivered an address, but that he also selected the menu for the dinner.

The year 1907, when the first of the Society's annual meetings was held, today appears to have been one of those moments in American history when we were concentrating upon building our American society, essentially untroubled by what took place beyond our borders. But the founders of this Society realized that the United States could not remain aloof from the world. It is one of the achievements of this Society that, from its inception, it has spread the realization that the United States cannot opt out of the community of nations—that international affairs are part of our national affairs.

Questions of war and peace occupied the Society at its first meeting. Among the subjects discussed were the possibility of the immunity of private property from belligerent seizure upon the high seas and whether trade in contraband of war was unneutral. Limitations upon recourse to force then proposed were embryonic, as is illustrated by the fact one topic for discussion related to restrictions upon the use of armed force in the collection of contract obligations. The distance between those ideas and the restrictions upon recourse to armed force contained in the Charter of the United Nations is vast. It is to these Charter restrictions—and their place in the practice and malpractice of States—that I shall address much of my remarks this evening.

Current United States policy arouses the criticism that it is at once too legal and too tough. Time was when the criticism of American concern with the legal element in international relations was that it led to softness—to a "legalistic-moralistic" approach to foreign affairs which conformed more to the ideal than to the real. Today, criticism of American attachment to the role of law is that it leads not to softness, but to severity. We are criticized not for sacrificing our national interests to international interests, but for endeavoring to impose the international interest upon other nations. We are criticized for acting as if the Charter of the United Nations means what it says. We are criticized for treating the statement of the law by the International Court of Justice as authoritative. We are criticized for taking collective security seriously.

This criticism is, I think, a sign of strength—of our strength, and of the strength of international law. It is a tribute to a blending of political purpose with legal ethic.

American foreign policy is at once principled and pragmatic. Its central objective is our national safety and well-being—to "secure the blessings of liberty to ourselves and our posterity." But we know we can no longer find security and well-being in defenses and policies which are confined to North America, or the Western Hemisphere, or the North Atlantic Community. This has become a very small planet. We have to be concerned with all of it—with all of its land, waters, atmosphere, and with surrounding space. We have a deep national interest in peace, the prevention of aggression, the faithful performance of agreements, the growth of international law. Our foreign policy is rooted in the profoundly practical realization that the Purposes and Principles of the United Nations Charter must animate the behavior of States, if mankind is to prosper or is even to survive. Or at least they must animate enough States with enough will and enough resources to see to it that others do not violate those rules with impunity.

The Preamble and Articles One and Two of the Charter set forth abiding purposes of American policy. This is not surprising, since we took the lead in drafting the Charter—at a time when the biggest war in history was still raging and we and others were thinking deeply about its frightful costs and the ghastly mistakes and miscalculations which led to it.

The kind of world we seek is the kind set forth in the opening sections of the Charter: a world community of independent states, each with the institutions of its own choice, but cooperating with one another to promote their mutual welfare . . . a world in which the use of force is effectively inhibited . . . a world of expanding human rights and well-being . . . a world of expanding international law . . . a world in which an agreement is a commitment and not just a tactic.

We believe that this is the sort of world a great majority of the governments of the world desire. We believe it is the sort of world man must achieve if he is not to perish. As I said on another occasion: "If once the rule of international law could be discussed with a certain condescension as a Utopian ideal, today it becomes an elementary practical necessity. *Pacta sunt servanda* now becomes the basis for survival."

Unhappily a minority of governments is committed to different ideas of the conduct and organization of human affairs. They are dedicated to the promotion of the Communist world revolution. And their doctrine justifies any technique, any ruse, any deceit, which contributes to that end. They may differ as to tactics from time to time. And the two principal Communist powers are competitors for the leadership of the world Communist movement. But both are committed to the eventual Communization of the entire world.

The overriding issue of our time is which concepts are to prevail: those set forth in the United Nations Charter or those proclaimed in the name of a world revolution.

The paramount commitment of the Charter is Article 2, paragraph 4, which reads: "All Members shall refrain in their international relations from the threat or use of force against the territorial integrity or political independence of any State, or in any other manner inconsistent with the Purposes of the United Nations."

This comprehensive limitation went beyond the Covenant of the League of Nations. This more sweeping commitment sought to apply a bitter lesson of the interwar period—that the threat or use of force, whether or not called "war," feeds on success. The indelible lesson of those years is that the time to stop aggression is at its very beginning.

The exceptions to the prohibitions on the use or threat of force were expressly set forth in the Charter. The use of force is legal:

. . . as a collective measure by the United Nations, or
. . . as action by regional agencies in accordance with Chapter VIII of the Charter, or
. . . in individual or collective self-defense.

When Article 2, paragraph 4 was written it was widely regarded as general international law, governing both Members and non-Members of the United Nations. And on the universal reach of the principle embodied in Article 2, paragraph 4, wide agreement remains. Thus, last year, a United Nations Special Committee on Principles of International Law concerning Friendly Relations and Cooperation among States met in Mexico City. All shades of United Nations opinion were represented. The Committee's purpose was to study and possibly to elaborate certain of those principles. The Committee debated much and agreed on little. But on one point, it reached swift and unanimous agreement: that all States, and not only all Members of the United Nations, are bound to refrain in their international relations from the threat or use of force against the territorial integrity or political independence of any State. Nonrecognition of the statehood of a political entity was held not to affect the international application of this cardinal rule of general international law.

But at this same meeting in Mexico City, Czechoslovakia, with the warm support of the Soviet Union and some other Members, proposed formally another exemption from the limitations on use of force. Their proposal stated that: "The prohibition of the use of force shall not affect . . . self-defense of nations against colonial domination in the exercise of the right of self-determination."

The United States is all for self-defense. We are against colonial domination—we led the way in throwing it off. We have long favored self-determination, in practice as well as in words—indeed, we favor it for the entire world, including the peoples behind the Iron and Bamboo curtains. But we could not accept the Czech proposal. And we were pleased that the Special Committee found the Czech proposal unacceptable.

The primary reason why we opposed that attempt to rewrite the Charter—apart from the inadmissibility of rewriting the Charter at all by such means—was that we knew the meaning behind the words. We knew that like so many statements from such sources, it used upside-down language—that it would in effect authorize a State to wage war, to use force internationally, as long as it claimed it was doing so to "liberate" somebody from "colonial domination." In short, the Czech resolution proposed to give to so-called "wars of national liberation" the same exemption from the limitation on the use of force which the Charter accords to defense against aggression.

What is a "war of national liberation"? It is, in essence, any war which furthers the Communist world revolution—what, in broader terms, the Communists have long referred to as a "just" war. The term "war of national liberation" is used not only to denote armed insurrection by people still under colonial rule— there are not many of those left outside the Communist world. It is used to denote any effort led by Communists to overthrow by force any non-Communist government.

Thus the war in South Vietnam is called a "war of national liberation." And those who would overthrow various other non-Communist governments in Asia, Africa, and Latin America are called the "forces of national liberation."

Nobody in his right mind would deny that Venezuela is not only a truly independent nation but that it has a government chosen in a free election. But the leaders of the Communist insurgency in Venezuela are described as leaders of a fight for "national liberation"—not only by themselves and by Castro and the Chinese Communists, but by the Soviet Communists.

A recent editorial in *Pravda* spoke of the "peoples of Latin America . . . marching firmly along the path of struggle for their national independence" and said: "the upsurge of the national liberation movement in Latin American countries has been to a great extent a result of the activities of Communist parties." It added: "The Soviet people have regarded and still regard it as their sacred duty to give support to the peoples fighting for their independence. True to their international duty the Soviet people have been and will remain on the side of the Latin American patriots."

In Communist doctrine and practice, a non-Communist government may be labeled and denounced as "colonialist," "reactionary," or a "puppet," and any State so labeled by the Communists automatically becomes fair game . . . while Communist intervention by force in non-Communist states is justified as "self-defense" or part of the "struggle against colonial domination." "Self-determination" seems to mean that any Communist nation can determine by itself that any non-Communist state is a victim of colonialist domination and therefore a justifiable target for a war of "liberation."

As the risks of overt aggression, whether nuclear or with conventional forces, have become increasingly evident, the Communists have put increasing stress on the "war of national liberation." The Chinese Communists have been more militant in language and behavior than the Soviet Communists. But the Soviet Communist leadership also has consistently proclaimed its commitment in principle to support wars of national liberation. This commitment was reaffirmed as recently as Monday of this week by Mr. Kosygin.

International law does not restrict internal revolution within a state, or revolution against colonial authority. But international law does restrict what third powers may lawfully do in support of insurrection. It is these restrictions which are challenged by the doctrine, and violated by the practice, of "wars of liberation."

It is plain that acceptance of the doctrine of "wars of liberation" would amount to scuttling the modern international law of peace which the Charter prescribes. And acceptance of the practice of "wars of liberation," as defined by the Communists, would mean the breakdown of peace itself.

Vietnam presents a clear current case of the lawful versus the unlawful use of force. I would agree with General Giap and other Communists that it is a test case for "wars of national liberation." We intend to meet that test.

Were the insurgency in South Vietnam truly indigenous and self-sustained, international law would not be involved. But the fact is that it receives vital external support—in organization and direction, in training, in men, in weapons and other supplies. That external support is unlawful, for a double reason. First, it contravenes general international law, which the United Nations Charter here expresses. Second, it contravenes particular international law: The 1954 Geneva Accords on Vietnam, and the 1962 Geneva Agreements on Laos.

In resisting the aggression against it, the Republic of Vietnam is exercising its right of self-defense. It called upon us and other states for assistance. And in the exercise of the right of collective self-defense under the United Nations Charter, we and other nations are providing such assistance.

The American policy of assisting South Vietnam to maintain its freedom was inaugurated under President Eisenhower, and continued under Presidents Kennedy and Johnson. Our assistance has been increased because the aggression from the North has been augmented. Our assistance now encompasses the bombing of North Vietnam. The bombing is designed to interdict, as far as possible, and to inhibit, as far as may be necessary, continued aggression against the Republic of Vietnam.

When that aggression ceases, collective measures in defense against it will cease. As President Johnson has declared: ". . . if that aggression is stopped, the people and Government of South Vietnam will be free to settle their own future, and the need for supporting American military action there will end."

The fact that the demarcation line between North and South Vietnam was intended to be temporary does not make the assault on South Vietnam any less of an aggression. The demarcation lines between North and South Korea and between East and West Germany are temporary. But that did not make the North Korean invasion of South Korea a permissible use of force.

Let's not forget the salient features of the 1962 agreements on Laos. Laos was to be independent and neutral. All foreign troops, regular or irregular, and other military personnel were to be withdrawn within seventy-five days, except a limited number of French instructors as requested by the Laos government. No arms were to be introduced into Laos except at the request of that government. The signatories agreed to refrain "from all direct or indirect interference in the internal affairs" of Laos. They promised also not to use Lao territory to intervene in the internal affairs of other countries—a stipulation that plainly prohibited the passage of arms and men from North Vietnam to South Vietnam by way of Laos. An International Control Commission of three was to assure compliance with the Agreements. And all the signatories promised to support a coalition government under Prince Souvanna Phouma.

What happened? The non-Communist elements complied. The Communists did not. At no time since that agreement was signed have either the Pathet Lao or the North Vietnam authorities complied with it. The North Vietnamese left several thousand troops there—the backbone of almost every Pathet Lao battalion. Use of the corridor through Laos to South Vietnam continued. And the Communists barred the areas under their control both to the government of Laos and the International Control Commission.

To revert to Vietnam: I continue to hear and see nonsense about the nature of the struggle there. I sometimes wonder at the gullibility of educated men and the stubborn disregard of plain facts by men who are supposed to be helping our young to learn—especially to learn how to think.

Hanoi has never made a secret of its designs. It publicly proclaimed in 1960 a renewal of the assault on South Vietnam. Quite obviously its hopes of taking over South Vietnam from within had withered to close to zero—and the remarkable economic and social progress of South Vietnam contrasted, most disagreeably for the North Vietnamese Communists, with their own miserable economic performance.

The facts about the external involvement have been documented in White Papers and other publications of the Department of State. The International Control Commission has held that there is evidence "beyond reasonable doubt" of North Vietnamese intervention.

There is no evidence that the Vietcong has any significant popular following in South Vietnam. It relies heavily on terror. Most of its reinforcements in recent months have been North Vietnamese from the North Vietnamese Army.

Let us be clear about what is involved today in Southeast Asia. We are not involved with empty phrases or conceptions which ride upon the clouds. We are talking about the vital national interests of the United States in the peace of the Pacific. We are talking about the appetite for aggression—an appetite which grows upon feeding and which is proclaimed to be insatiable. We are talking about the safety of nations with whom we are allied—and the integrity of the American commitment to join in meeting attack. It is true that we also believe that every small state has a right to be unmolested by its neighbors even though it is within reach of a great power. It is true that we are committed to general principles of law and procedure which reject the idea that men and arms can be sent freely across frontiers to absorb a neighbor. But underlying the general principles is the harsh reality that our own security is threatened by those who would embark upon a course of aggression whose announced ultimate purpose is our own destruction. Once again we hear expressed the views which cost the men of my generation a terrible price in World War II. We are told that Southeast Asia is far away—but so were Manchuria and Ethiopia. We are told that if we insist that someone stop shooting that is asking them for unconditional surrender. We are told that perhaps the aggressor will be content with just one more bite. We are told that if we prove faithless on one commitment that perhaps others would believe us about other commitments in other places. We are told that if we stop resisting that perhaps the other side will have a change of heart. We were asked to stop hitting bridges and radar sites and ammunition depots without requiring that the other side stop its slaughter of thousands of civilians and its bombings of schools and hotels and hospitals and railways and buses.

Surely we have learned over the past three decades that the acceptance of aggression leads only to a sure catastrophe. Surely we have learned that the aggressor must face the consequences of his action and be saved from the frightful miscalculation that brings all to ruin. It is the purpose of law to guide men away from such events, to establish rules of conduct which are deeply rooted in the reality of experience.

Before closing, I should like to turn away from the immediate difficulties and dangers of the situation in Southeast Asia and remind you of the dramatic progress that shapes and is being shaped by expanding international law.

A "common law of mankind"—to use the happy phrase of your distinguished colleague, Wilfred Jenks—is growing as the world shrinks, and as the vistas of space expand. This year is, by proclamation of the General Assembly, International Cooperation Year, a year "to direct attention to the common interests of mankind and to accelerate the joint efforts being undertaken to further them." Those common interests are enormous and intricate, and the joint efforts which further them are developing fast, although perhaps not fast enough.

In the nineteenth century, the United States attended an average of one international conference a year. Now we attend nearly 600 a year. We are party to 4,300 treaties and other international agreements in force. Three fourths of these were signed in the last twenty-five years. Our interest in the observance of all of these treaties and agreements is profound, whether the issue is peace in Laos, or the payment of United Nations assessments, or the allocation of radio frequencies, or the application of airline safeguards, or the control of illicit traffic in narcotics, or any other issue which States have chosen to regulate through the law-making process. The writing of international cooperation into international law is meaningful only if the law is obeyed—and only if the international institutions which administer and develop the law function in accordance with agreed procedures, until the procedures are changed.

Everything suggests that the rate of growth in international law—like the rate of change in almost every other field these days—is rising at a very steep angle.

In recent years the law of the sea has been developed and codified—but it first evolved in a leisurely fashion over the centuries. International agreements to regulate aerial navigation had to be worked out within the period of a couple of decades. Now, within the first few years of man's adventures in outer space, we are deeply involved in the creation of international institutions, regulations, and law to govern this effort.

Already the United Nations has developed a set of legal principles to govern the use of outer space and declared celestial bodies free from national appropriation.

Already nations, including the United States and the Soviet Union, have agreed not to orbit weapons of mass destruction in outer space.

Already the Legal Subcommittee of the United Nations Committee on Outer Space is formulating international agreements on liability for damage caused by the reentry of objects launched into outer space and on rescue and return of astronauts and space objects.

Already the first international sounding rocket range has been established in India and is being offered for United Nations sponsorship.

To make orderly space exploration possible at this stage, the International Telecommunications Union had to allocate radio frequencies for the purpose.

To take advantage of weather reporting and forecasting potential of observation satellites, married to computer technology, the World Meteorological Organization is creating a vast system of data acquisition, analysis, and distribution which depends entirely on international agreement, regulation and standards.

And to start building a single global communications satellite system, we have created a novel international institution in which a private American corporation shares ownership with forty-five governments.

This is but part of the story of how the pace of discovery and invention forces us to reach out for international agreement, to build international institutions, to do things in accordance with an expanding international and transnational law.

Phenomenal as the growth of treaty obligations is, the true innovation of twentieth century international law lies more in the fact that we have nearly eighty international institutions which are capable of carrying out those obligations.

It is important that the processes and products of international cooperation be understood and appreciated; and it is important that their potential be much further developed. It is also important that the broader significance of the contributions of international cooperation to the solving of international problems of an economic, social, scientific and humanitarian character not be overestimated. For all the progress of peace could be incinerated in war.

Thus the control of force in international relations remains the paramount problem which confronts the diplomat and the lawyer—and the man in the street and the man in the rice field. Most of mankind is not in an immediate position to grapple very directly with that problem, but the problem is no less crucial. The responsibility of those, in your profession and mine, who do grapple with it is the greater. I am happy to acknowledge that this Society, in thinking and debating courageously and constructively about the conditions of peace, continues to make its unique contribution and to make it well.

FAREWELLS TO THE GIANTS

ADDRESS AT THE MEMORIAL SERVICE FOR
SIR WINSTON CHURCHILL [1]

ADLAI E. STEVENSON [2]

Sir Winston Churchill died January 24, 1965. With his passing the world lost, by fairly general agreement, the greatest orator of modern times. "His speeches will live," said the *Times* (London), "and not only in the memory of his contemporaries still under the spell of glowing phrases."

> Never has the spoken word taken the colour of a greater cause or served it more decisively. In the hour when all but courage failed, Churchill made courage conscious of itself, plumed it with defiance, and rendered it invincible.

Sir Winston was one of those rare persons shared by many nations. Americans regarded him as their own, as witnessed by conferral upon him on April 9, 1963, of honorary citizenship. His addresses were in the best Western tradition, and two of them—the speech to Congress on December 26, 1941 and the Fulton, Missouri, speech of March 5, 1946—seem as much "American oratory" as the addresses of our own leaders during and after the Second World War. As C. L. Sulzberger of the New York *Times* remarked: "Of no other contemporary can it be said with such affectionate truth: It has been splendid to be aboard the earth with him."

A memorial service for Sir Winston was held January 28, 1965, at the National Cathedral, Washington, D.C. It was wholly fitting that an American with a felicity of expression comparable to Sir Winston's perform the last offices. The late Ambassador Adlai E. Stevenson, United States Representative to the United Nations, pronounced the eulogy on the voice, now silenced, "that led nations, raised armies, inspired victories and blew fresh courage into the hearts of men."

Today we meet in sadness to mourn one of the world's greatest citizens. Sir Winston Churchill is dead. The voice that led

---

[1] Text furnished by Margaret L. Gerstle, public affairs officer, United States Mission to the United Nations, with permission for this reprint.

[2] For biographical note, see Appendix.

nations, raised armies, inspired victories and blew fresh courage into the hearts of men is silenced. We shall hear no longer the remembered eloquence and wit, the old courage and defiance, the robust serenity of indomitable faith. Our world is thus poorer, our political dialogue is diminished and the sources of public inspiration run more thinly for all of us. There is a lonesome place against the sky.

So we are right to mourn. Yet, in contemplating the life and spirit of Winston Churchill, regrets for the past seem singularly insufficient. One rather feels a sense of thankfulness and encouragement that throughout so long a life, such a full measure of power, virtuosity, mastery and zest played over our human scene.

Contemplating this completed career, we feel a sense of enlargement and exhilaration. Like the grandeur and power of the masterpieces of art and music, Churchill's life uplifts our hearts and fills us with fresh revelation of the scale and reach of human achievement. We may be sad; but we rejoice as well, as all must rejoice when they "now praise famous men" and see in their lives the full splendor of our human estate.

And regrets for the past are insufficient for another reason. Churchill, the historian, felt the continuity of past and present, the contribution which mighty men and great events make to the future experience of mankind; history's "flickering lamp" lights up the past and sends its gleams into the future. So to the truth of Santayana's dictum, "Those who will not learn from the past are destined to repeat it," Churchill's whole life was witness. It was his lonely voice that in the thirties warned Britain and Europe of the follies of playing all over again the tragedy of disbelief and of unpreparedness. And in the time of Britain's greatest trial he mobilized the English language to inspire his people to historic valor to save their beleaguered island. It was his voice again that helped assemble the great coalition that has kept peace steady through the last decades.

He once said: "We cannot say the past is past without surrendering the future." So today the "past" of his life and his achievement are a guide and light to the future. And we can only properly mourn and celebrate this mighty man by heeding him as a living influence in the unfolding dramas of our days ahead.

What does he tell us for this obscure future whose outlines we but dimly discern? First, I believe, he would have us reaffirm his serene faith in human freedom and dignity. The love of freedom was not for him an abstract thing but a deep conviction that the uniqueness of man demands a society that gives his capacities full scope. It was, if you like, an aristocratic sense of the fullness and value of life. But he was a profound democrat, and the cornerstone of his political faith, inherited from a beloved father, was the simple maxim—"Trust the people." Throughout his long career, he sustained his profound concern for the well-being of his fellow citizens.

Instinctively, profoundly, the people trusted "good old Winnie," the peer's son. He could lead them in war because he had respected them in peace. He could call for their greatest sacrifices for he knew how to express their deepest dignity—citizens of equal value and responsibility in a free and democratic state.

His crucial part in the founding of the United Nations expressed his conviction that the Atlantic Charter he and President Roosevelt audaciously proclaimed at the height of Hitler's victories would have to be protected throughout the world by institutions embodying the ideal of the rule of law and international cooperation.

For him, humanity, its freedom, its survival, towered above pettier interests—national rivalries, old enmities, the bitter disputes of race and creed. "In victory—magnanimity; in peace—good will" were more than slogans. In fact, his determination to continue in politics after his defeat in 1945 and to toil on in office in the 1950's to the limit of health and endurance sprang from his belief that he could still "bring nearer that lasting peace which the masses of people of every race and in every land so fervently desire." The great soldier and strategist was a man of peace—and for the most simple reason—his respect, his faith, his compassion for the family of man.

His career saw headlong success and headlong catastrophe. He was at the height. He was flung to the depths. He saw his worst prophecies realized, his worst forebodings surpassed. Yet throughout it all his zest for living, gallantry of spirit, wry humor and compassion for human frailties took all grimness out of his fortitude and all pomposity out of his dedication.

Churchill's sense of the incomparable value and worth of human existence never faltered, nor the robust courage with which he lived it to the full. In the darkest hour, the land could still be bright, and for him hopes were not deceivers. It was forever fear that was the dupe. Victory at last would always lie with life and faith, for Churchill saw beyond the repeated miseries of human frailty the larger vision of mankind's "upward ascent towards his distant goal."

He used to say that he was half American and all English. But we put that right when the Congress made him an honorary citizen of his mother's native land and we shall always claim a part of him. I remember once years ago during a long visit at his country house he talked proudly of his American Revolutionary ancestors and happily of his boyhood visits to the United States. As I took my leave I said I was going back to London to speak to the English Speaking Union and asked if he had any message for them. "Yes," he said, "tell them that you bring greetings from an English Speaking Union." And I think that perhaps it was to the relations of the United Kingdom and the United States that he made his finest contribution.

In the last analysis, all the zest and life and confidence of this incomparable man sprang, I believe, not only from the rich endowment of his nature, but also from a profound and simple faith in God. In the prime of his powers, confronted with the apocalyptic risks of annihilation, he said serenely: "I do not believe that God has despaired of his children." In old age, as the honors and excitements faded, his resignation had a touching simplicity: "Only faith in a life after death in a brighter world where dear ones will meet again—only that and the measured tramp of time can give consolation."

The great aristocrat, the beloved leader, the profound historian, the gifted painter, the superb politician, the lord of language, the orator, the wit,—yes, and the dedicated bricklayer— behind all of them was the man of simple faith, steadfast in defeat, generous in victory, resigned in age, trusting in a loving Providence and committing his achievements and his triumphs to a higher power.

Like the patriarchs of old, he waited on God's judgment and it could be said of him—as of the immortals that went before him —that God "magnified him in the fear of his enemies and with his words he made prodigies to cease. He glorified him in the sight of kings and gave him commandments in the sight of his people. He showed him his Glory and sanctified him in his faith. . . ."

HERBERT CLARK HOOVER [3]

D. ELTON TRUEBLOOD [4]

Herbert Clark Hoover died October 20, 1964, at the age of 90. Thirty-first President of the United States, he outlived the mistaken legend that he was somehow personally responsible for the economic distress of the late 1920's. He was a selfless man whose concern for mankind, as evidenced strikingly by his relief work from 1914 to 1923, prompted Dr. Frederick Brown Harris, chaplain of the United States Senate, to salute him as "one who brought sustenance to more starving humans than any other man who has ever walked this earth." Never, said Brooks Atkinson, has there been "a better American than Herbert Hoover."

At the simple funeral rites in West Branch, Iowa, on October 25, Dr. D. Elton Trueblood, Quaker theologian and friend of President Hoover, spoke briefly of "the last of the famous pioneers," of the man who "demonstrated an ethic which is identical with that which made America great."

We have gathered today to honor one of the great men of the twentieth century. His is the story of what is best in the American heritage. He bears witness to a way of life which we seldom demonstrate, but which is infinitely precious in that it provides a standard by which we may judge our relative failures, as well as our relative successes. In so far as his is the kind of life we truly prize, the basic orientation of the Republic is likely to be sound. Therefore we perform a service when we try to make clear the nature of the heritage which Herbert Clark Hoover, the thirty-first President of the United States of America, has represented with unusual fidelity.

First, there is the beginning which combines reverence, frugality and toil. Herbert Hoover belongs to the procession of hard-working and God-loving Quaker pioneers who crossed the

[3] Text furnished by Dr. Trueblood, with permission for this reprint.
[4] For biographical note, see Appendix.

nation in great steps, establishing strong communities at each point. West Milton, Ohio, and West Branch, Iowa, were important stopping places as the Hoovers moved from the Atlantic to the Pacific. The Quaker cemetery near the west branch of the Miami River and the simple frame birthplace at West Branch, Iowa, are potent symbols of something precious in American history. They are symbols of men close to the soil and close to Almighty God who made it. It is important to remember that the life of toil and reverence led naturally to the life of learning, so that schools were set up at each stopping place along the way. That Herbert Hoover, as a boy of 17, should be attracted to Stanford University in its opening year was, therefore, in no way surprising.

The expectation of hard work carried over into the life of learning in those glorious years when Stanford was new. By amazing good fortune the Quaker boy was guided, not only into the study of geology, but into the study of Latin under a man as remarkable as Professor Augustus T. Murray. The result was an unending spiritual influence, which reached its climax in the days in the White House.

Herbert Hoover's work as a geologist and mining engineer was brilliantly successful, but the public judgment is right in thinking of this vocational chapter as only a preparation for larger public work. The great days at the end of the First World War, and immediately afterward, when Herbert Hoover, in his mission of compassion, was the most influential man in Europe, constituted, not an interlude in Herbert Hoover's career, but a logical fulfillment.

All along, the heritage to which he was being faithful was one in which public service is intrinsic. The consciously nourished ideal required every Christian to find, on his pilgrim-way, the life to which God had called him, whether humble or exalted. It included a conception in which duty could be mentioned without self-consciousness and without apology. It required of each person that he should show diligence in his calling, that he should practice frugality and simplicity, and that he should accept responsibility for some unique contribution to the total community.

The most important thing to say about Herbert Hoover is that he has demonstrated an ethic which is identical with that which made America great. There are some who suppose that we have outgrown it, or that we ought to outgrow it, but a life like that which we honor today is the best refutation of their position.

It is not unreasonable to see Herbert Hoover's life in six major chapters. These six are as follows: 1, Boy in Iowa and Oregon; 2, Student at Stanford; 3, Engineer in various countries; 4, Director of relief; 5, Statesman; 6, Elder.

It might be supposed that the last of these chapters would be an anticlimax, but it has not been so. Instead, his influence has gone on from strength to strength. He became the very idea of the elder statesman, writing much, speaking seldom, counseling untold numbers of men and women and standing as a symbol of moral strength.

All knew that there was at least one great man in America who stood above the possibility of corruption and self-seeking. All recognized that he was one who had never sought personal gain or even payment for his public service. As the years went on, after the end of the White House days, through the great depression, through the Second World War, and through the years which succeeded that war, there was probably no thoughtful person in the United States who did not come to see the unfairness of the judgment of those who had blamed Mr. Hoover for what was in reality a world-wide economic storm. In his magnificent patience Mr. Hoover did not even worry about the outcome. He knew that he had been right, he knew that he had been unjustly blamed, and by a wonderful grace he lived long enough to see the time when what had been a problem was a problem no longer. Indeed, as we see the events of thirty-five years ago in perspective, it is obvious that the critics have been more hurt than the criticized. This is particularly true of those who tried to raise their own public stature by seeking to harm that of Mr. Hoover. These critics now stand out clearly for all to see; and the public has made its judgment.

The six chapters are now over, and in one sense the volume is complete, but there is another sense in which it is still going on. Herbert Hoover will be remembered as long as the American dream is cherished because he is, to such a great extent, the last of the famous pioneers. He represents the westward trek; he represents dignified simplicity; he represents to a remarkable degree the unity of a faith which expresses itself in compassionate service to mankind. He has worked hard; he has been very brave; he has endured. How appropriate that what is mortal of him should finally rest, after all his struggles and his victories, in his native soil, mid-way in the western trek and near the middle of North America. He never wavered from the living faith in Jesus Christ which was indigenous to his heritage, and in which he lived and served and died.

The story is a great one and it is a good one. It is essentially a story that is triumphant. Therefore it is reasonable that today our mood should be one of rejoicing. This is not a time for tears. This corruption has put on incorruption; this mortal has put on immortality; death is swallowed up in victory. Thanks be to God, which giveth us the victory through our Lord, Jesus Christ.

SOME THOUGHTS ON MEN AND INSTITUTIONS

THE LIBRARY AND THE CHAPEL STAND SIDE BY SIDE [1]

ROBERT F. GOHEEN [2]

At the beginning of the academic year at many institutions, students and faculty join in what is variously but perhaps most frequently called orientation exercises. The activities include an address to the incoming or returning students by the president or some other noted scholar from the academic community. Usually the speech has a distinctive character. It is partly informational, partly inspirational, and mildly hortatory.

This special occasion has produced first-rate addresses. Many readers have doubtless been introduced to Edmund Sears Morgan's "What Every Yale Freshman Should Know" in which the student is urged to develop a curiosity for truth and a competence to communicate whatever truth is found. Similarly, Charles D. O'Connell, in his "Not All Change Is Growth," advised the incoming freshmen at the University of Chicago that a proper education involves the search for knowledge and understanding. "To its pursuit," he remarked, "I hope you will bring curiosity, flexibility, humility, a respect for ideas, and the saving grace of a sense of humor."

Robert F. Goheen's address properly joins the circle of select statements. A distinguished classical scholar, the president of Princeton University, he gave this speech at the opening exercises on September 20, 1964.

Long-held and most fitting custom has brought us together this morning—members of the Trustees, the faculty, students, administrators, neighbors, and friends—to mark the opening of the academic year in a service of worship. I follow custom, too, in directing my remarks particularly to those undergraduates who have freshly joined the University.

[1] Text furnished by Dan D. Coyle, assistant to President Goheen, with permission for this reprint.

[2] For biographical note, see Appendix.

For you of the Class of 1968, this service marks a new stage in your lives. Your years of secondary school, your admission to Princeton, your first few days of settling in amid different sights and sounds upon this campus—all this has been prelude to your assuming a new role. Like the young men who donned gowns 500 years ago to enter the medieval universities, and like those who will follow you here and at other institutions in years to come, you are about to become different from what you were; you are about to become university men.

As we hail this prospect, let us not forget its sometimes sad corollary—namely, that the experience can mean much or little. It can deepen and broaden your lives, or it can pass over you lightly and leave you largely unscathed. Indeed, I recall one of last year's seniors wryly regretting that he had not given his studies a full chance in just these words, "I guess I never let myself be more than superficially wounded."

Princeton holds out to you a rich and challenging curriculum, first-rate teaching, situations conducive to active learning and growth; but it is you yourselves who will determine whether your "wounds" are deep or superficial. That will hinge upon what is inside you in ability, in sensitivity, in aspiration, and in courage —upon what of all this you bring to bear on your own learning and growing.

Most of you will, I trust, be deeply influenced and for the good. For, you will know by now that a university education is not simply a process of pouring in knowledge, that you are not here to be sponges, but to seek, to inquire, to react, and to grow. Late though the hour is, if any of you has come to Princeton hoping only to accumulate knowledge, I would advise you to begin immediate negotiations with some other sort of institution where you can attach yourself to a pipeline of inanimate learning and become full, like a storage tank, sealed by a diploma, and otherwise useless.

If you are to be influenced here, if you are to react, in significant ways, you must make connection with the electricity in the intellectual life of Princeton; and I warn you that the current is high voltage. It does not merely tingle; it can shock. It involves an encounter with facts, ideas, arguments, and even teachers who will puzzle, irritate, and upset you. Many things you have taken for granted will be challenged. Much that you have assumed to be certain you will discover to be highly uncertain, as is so much of life. Learning to respect data, learning to explore concepts in depth, learning to take on to yourself the hard ways of dispassionate, disciplined thought: all this will not be a soothing experience. It is not intended to be. Yet, you have it in your power to do these things and more; even as you could also (but with much less chance of staying here) opt to be passive, to be like balls on a pool table, shoved around and shunted into side pockets.

Now, the deans seated behind me may be stirring uneasily while I urge on you self-propelling endeavor and vigorous responses; for, students can react in many ways, and some of their activities do not make the proctors' lives easier. I was reminded the other day of an old lamentation:

> Our youths now love luxury. They have bad manners, contempt for authority, disrespect for older people. They no longer rise when their elders enter the room. They contradict their parents, . . . and tyrannize their teachers.

The significant thing about this set of observations is that it was made not in America in the era of the Beatles and the Birchers but (reportedly) by Socrates in the fifth century B.C., the so-called Golden Age of Greek culture. Young men always will kick up their heels. Their deportment probably never has perfectly satisfied older generations.

Growing through such phases is largely a matter of time and reasonable self-restraint on the part (insofar as they can manage it) both of elders and of juniors. Accordingly, in the area of conduct the University asks simply that you order your lives as gentlemen. The expectation is well summed up in the first clause of the pledge under the Honor System, "I pledge my honor as a gentleman. . . ." "I pledge": the commitment is one's own and the emphasis is on a sense of personal integrity which others can trust. "Honor": that difficult term which embraces so much, but especially an unwillingness to be corrupted and a willingness to accept trust. Finally, the word "gentleman": the roots of the concept reach far back in Western history, wherein slowly, but imperfectly, standards of decency have been evolved (and are still evolving) as against the savagery and selfishness which continue to be such potent forces in the lives and affairs of men.

In moving into these topics, have I strayed from the idea I set forward at the start of these remarks: the significance of becoming a university man? I think not. The transaction of the world's business requires mental capacity in large measure and in many ways, but it requires also more than this. In the business of building a life, intellectual and moral obligations are inextricably connected; and when one enters a university, he goes upon a moral quest as well as upon an intellectual one. Indeed, just as you will find that so-called "academic questions" are seldom purely "academic" (in the common and erroneous sense of that word, connoting a divorce from life), so you will find that issues of purpose and value cannot be disposed of by the cold eye of the quantifying intellect, but remain vital and insistent for the thoughtful individual. The house of intellect is raised, sustained, enlarged, and lighted not by the mind alone but by efforts of will and powers of spirit as well—in the wonderful words of Baron von Hugel, by such qualities as "candor, moral courage, intellectual honesty, scrupulous accuracy, chivalrous fairness, endless docility to facts, disinterested collaboration, unconquerable hopefulness, perseverance, manly renunciation of popularity and easy honors, love of bracing labor, and strengthening solitude."

Now, I grant that such phrases are not precise: yet, I hope we can agree that for each person there is an unavoidable range of concern that reaches beyond himself. When fully realized, it includes fairness and kindness and tolerance toward one's fellow men; allegiance to principles and to ideals; acknowledgment of one's humanity; and a sense of that which is ineffably holy, of

God who is the source of our lives. Men may dedicate much or little, but the need to reach outward and the obligation to give of themselves beyond themselves are always with them. So will it be with you as university men, through all the acts of your lives here, in all your dealings, whether in the classroom, the dormitory, or in casual encounters on the campus. No day will pass in which you will not make some moral decision—will not act upon (or fail to act upon) a principle or a conviction that tests your integrity and worth. You are free to deny the obligation, to evade it, to slight it, or to ignore it; but it will be there. Whether you act upon it or not, it will be there. Others can help you see it and perhaps understand its dimensions and importance better; but in the last analysis you must recognize such responsibilities yourself, define them with your own mind, feel them in your own heart.

In this aspect of your lives the University has a deep concern which may not always be shown overtly and obviously. For the most part your professors and advisers will be engaged in helping you to grow and deepen intellectually. Though by no means their entire interest and obligation, that is their primary business with you. In so far as it is separable, which is only in part, the work of maturing and shaping the moral and spiritual structure of your lives must be more largely your own affair. But do not be misled into thinking that Princeton has no concern. As you come to know members of the faculty well—and it will be your fault, not theirs, if you do not—you will find that the University's objective is the advancement of knowledge and of men. Our commitment to investigation and the pursuit of truth is to help lighten up the conditions of human life, and we seek to enhance the creative capacity of individuals like yourselves so that you both may live fuller lives and better see and serve the good of all.

You are the first students to enter Princeton free of a requirement of attendance at services of worship. Yet, *Dei sub numine viget* stands as Princeton's firm motto and conviction. As individuals and as a group, you have been granted this freedom in the belief that the majority of you will seek the Chapel or the church of your choice the more freely and sincerely, and therefore will gain the more from them.

There was of course a time when Chapel attendance twice a day was part of the making of a university man. We have now moved into an era when such a requirement no longer seems appropriate or effective. But this does not mean that we abandon religious faith, or our sense of the importance of faith to every life. Quite the contrary, we hold that without a religious dimension there is no fullness in being, and only shallow and illusionary light upon the deep, insistent final issues of meaning and purpose. Therefore I hope that you will use this freedom as every freedom should be used, not as an excuse for lazy disinterest but as a context in which to exercise significant judgment and thoughtful choice.

The Library and the Chapel stand side by side in Princeton to tell us of the need in our lives and in the world of those precious ingredients, mind and spirit, intelligence and faith. Among your fellows and among the citizens of this country there will be those who will be scornful of the one and skeptical of the other. They will resist ideas, moral or otherwise; or they will resist convictions. Some will hold up tight codes and narrow prejudices as the only road to salvation and desperate bulwark against an open, searching mind. Others will argue that anything goes, that nothing really matters, that what anyone does is all right so long as he is not caught. But, like anything cheap, neither of these reductive propositions holds up. The genuinely examined life will follow no such tawdry or such bigoted patterns. If the experience of mankind has taught anything, it is that reason and morality—by which I mean for the individual mind and spirit and will and conscience, all seriously cultivated and deeply exercised together—must go with us as guides to lead us above the choking ignorance and ravenous self-interests that rob life of its meaning and finest potential.

Our nation has been through a summer of grave moral strain and disorder, and the end is nowhere yet in sight. Meanwhile the country has moved into an election campaign where slogans are being offered in place of ideas and rampant emotional appeals in place of reason. How great is our need for clear sight and a sense of balance was shown both in San Francisco and in Atlantic City during the summer months. And how desperately we need common standards of decency and citizenship was made grimly evident in such far-flung cities as Jacksonville and Rochester and (so ironically) the two Philadelphias. Can we wonder that we are being anxiously watched by a nervous world, when so much depends upon our ability as a people to be perspicacious and firm in the cause of freedom and justice.

When we peer over the abyss, and wonder whether mankind can marshal the intelligence, the spiritual sensitivity, and the moral strength necessary to avoid descent to the brutality which is pictured so tellingly in Golding's *Lord of the Flies* and which ever lurks just below the surface of even men's most civilized accomplishments, then with trepidation we fasten, in Housman's phrase, "our hands upon our hearts." But we can turn to the enduring example of universities like ours and to the symbolism of the Library and the Chapel as roads which remain open and which, because they demand of us our best, still offer much hope. They suggest a more humane and beatific aspiration than anything so far achieved upon earth. They invite you to set your course to ends that are worth our striving.

CHALLENGES AND EXCELLENCES [3]

JOHN HAY WHITNEY [4]

The civil rights movement of the sixties furnishes many acute reminders of another crusade in American history in which reformers and agitators sought to realize the basic freedoms to which all men are properly entitled. These were the abolitionists—Wendell Phillips, William Lloyd Garrison, Frederick Douglass, Charles G. Finney, Angelina Grimké, and others—whose dedication and moral fervor did much no doubt to hasten social progress. While they were often criticized for their tactics, and even today the epithets of radicalism and immoderation are sometimes assigned to their methods, they fought the battle with laudable zeal and a sort of intellectual indifference toward their detractors.

Students of public address invariably associate Wendell Phillips' name with Elijah P. Lovejoy, who was murdered in Alton, Illinois, on November 7, 1837, while guarding the printing press of his Alton *Observer* in which he had advocated the abolition of slavery. On December 8, at Faneuil Hall, Boston, Phillips delivered his speech on the murder of Lovejoy. One of our most fiery statements in defense of a free press, it catapulted Phillips into national prominence as an anti-slavery orator. For the next twenty-five years he kept the image of the victim's muted abolitionist press in public memory.

Elijah P. Lovejoy graduated from Maine's Colby College (then Waterville) in 1826. In 1952 the College set up an award to be conferred annually upon a newspaperman whose "integrity, craftsmanship and character . . . continues the heritage of fearlessness and freedom of Elijah Lovejoy." At a convocation on November 12, John Hay Whitney was awarded an honorary degree and named the 1964 Elijah Parish Lovejoy Fellow. In his address, the editor in chief and publisher of the New York *Herald Tribune* spoke of the challenges and excellences of modern journalism, citing as the newspaper's task "to cut through the junk in the public mind by seeking the order that underlies the clutter of small events." In taking a stand "in an embattled culture," and making "sense of it all," the newspaper should "winnow out of the apparent what is the real" and "cede to television and radio the mere repetition of activities and . . . look behind the bare event for meanings."

[3] Text furnished by Mr. Whitney, with permission for this reprint.
[4] For biographical note, see Appendix.

In some cultures it is believed possible to gain merit by sleeping on beds of nails or tattooing the body. In ours, possibly as the result of confining religion to Sunday sermons, there seems to be a belief that merit attaches to the occasional public address. The teacher is neglected, the haranguer from street corners is ignored. But the man who speaks to the testimonial dinner or delivers the memorial lecture, and the audience that settles quietly to listen to him, both take deep draughts of comfort in doing good.

Oddly, there may be some truth in it. It forces people like me to come to grips with the ideas that lie behind our daily actions and if the audience can rise to a decent skepticism about the whole process, it can use the opportunity to judge those ideas.

Let us begin with the skepticism. A lot of nonsense is talked about newspapers and publishing—not least by newspapermen and publishers. Quite simply, I am proud to be here. My predecessors at these lectures have been eminent men who have all worked long at their profession. But I think it is clear that though I have worked at journalism, I am here today primarily because I am a millionaire.

It is not polite to go into this sort of thing. Heaven knows it is not comfortable. This was brought home recently when I read about my wealth, my homes and my possessions in *Fortune* magazine. But in all honesty, I know, as you should, that I am the fourteenth annual Elijah Parish Lovejoy lecturer here today because five years ago I was able to buy the New York *Herald Tribune* and I have since been able to finance it and help it find new paths in American journalism.

I did not do so in hopes of finding fame and fortune. Nor did I do it, as Lord Beaverbrook used to claim on his own behalf, in order to find a vehicle for political propaganda—although my newspaper and I share a view of life we like to call Independent Republican. As for business reasons, well, it may be that there are worse investments in this country than running a competitive morning newspaper in a busy, bitterly competitive, sophisticated town, but I have never run across one.

I did it because I had to. I did it because all my life, in one way and another, I have been involved in—horrible word—"communications." I did it because we live in a time when there are challenges only a newspaper can meet and excellences only a newspaper can set and because I believe we cannot let the world go by default to the dullards. In short, I did it because when the opportunity arose to buy the *Herald Tribune*, I looked back on my life and found that I was an apprentice journalist.

The process has been a long one and I could have spoken on some other occasion—indeed, I have spoken—as a man from another career.

I made movies once, with David O. Selznick, when there was fun and adventure in the enterprise. We made *Gone with the Wind* and other films, talking about them as "only entertainment," and looked back to discover that we helped shape an art form not only reflecting but in a way influencing our times.

After the war, with J. H. Whitney and Company, I started a venture capital enterprise that tried to turn ideas into industries. What we found, instead of the post-war slump and recession that everyone had predicted, was an eagerness to translate the new technology into new products. In a small way, we were creating the physical face of the world you and I now live in.

And I was an ambassador. In a part of the world I love, where my education was shaped and many of my closest friendships made, I was charged with interpreting to Britain what was best in America. There I found that you can so hold the values of your life, like playing cards, so close to your chest, that in working out the game you forget exactly what they are; you don't see them; they are part of you. But asked to explain the hand, you can look again and name them—values *and* cards.

By that path, I came here today, to talk about journalism. And where are we?

We are, I think, at a point where to venture into a competitive market requires a great deal of money or a great variety of resources. And the profit still lies in monopoly situations where, too often, there is more income than excellence. It becomes proper to ask whether newspapers are not, perhaps, old-fashioned squares in a life which is bewilderingly complex. It is also proper to ask whether, perhaps, the newspaper's day has come and gone and television and news magazines are here to bury it; whether age has not made it infirm and challenge timid; whether there is any excuse for anyone bothering any more with the craft of journalism except as an aid for the professional few who need technical information and the bored many who need a hiding place on the commuter trains and a handy place to find the department store ads.

Consider that we are gathered here as survivors of the recent political campaign. To some—indeed as I read the reports from around the country, to a very great many—its chief characteristic was that it was boring. In the hurried reporters' great cliché, it was full of sound and fury signifying little.

Not so.

For our history and our future, it was historic almost to the pitch of high tragedy. To see nothing but its boredom is to confuse lack of suspense with lack of meaning. Lacking suspense, lacking also the sharp definition of great issues we had been told to expect from the man who was going to provide a choice not an echo, it seemed pointless.

But throughout the early fall we were dealing with the temporary, we hope, disintegration of a great party. In the broad sweep before us any citizen could sense the nation was at a political watershed. And we saw a vote not for but against—against Senator Goldwater and occasionally against President Johnson.

This was the reality behind the daily appearance of press conferences and midwest swings, television appearances and behind-the-scenes briefings. This is the reality that will make the stuff of history books.

Journalism's pride is to call itself the annotator of instant history, the source material for later interpretation. But what newspapers in the United States printed the reality instead of only the appearance? Which headlines are not headed for the forgotten addenda of some future doctoral thesis?

Again, we had a campaign remarkable in the volume of its reporting, an election night remarkable in the speed of that reporting. We had more statistics more quickly available for more interpretation than at any time in our history. In some instances, there were barely fifteen minutes between the close of the polls and the announcement of who won. And who did all this? The newspapers? Hardly. The New York *Times* allied itself with CBS for the night; the *Herald Tribune* allied itself with NBC and the wire services pooled with both.

And almost uniformly, using the computers that television brought and the speed that television demanded; faced with the drama that television could produce for a new generation of Americans, the newspapers of this country—with a few minor typographical innovations—produced the same morning-after papers they produced a generation ago.

Indeed, we seem to have lost something: a spirit of independence, a spirit of our own ferocity, that has made us captive to the press release and the gentlemanly code of going to great lengths to avoid embarrassing anyone.

In one way, life has been made incomparably easier for today's reporter than it was a generation ago. There is no corporation that does not strive to produce news about itself. There are few bureaus that do not employ a briefing officer. There is no reporter who could not produce enough copy simply by collecting what is given away.

But the privileges we claim for ourselves at every step are based on the old conception of ourselves as the public's watchdog, as the men a little outside our society, measuring it with a pinch of skepticism. If the press conferences become less productive because they are more polite, the fault may be ours. And it's a fault that cuts across the whole of newspaper life. Reporters who don't believe it is right to compete for news; editors who hesitate to offend an administration or take issue with it because to do so may be uncomfortable; publishers whose political friends become sacred items of news.

To be fair is not enough any more. We must be ferociously fair, the way a computer can be on election night when it tells you facts you would rather not know—but tells them nevertheless, with the emphasis they deserve.

I am a man involved in more directorships and enterprises than many of my fellow citizens. I have political as well as other friendships. But the day my newspaper begins to cease troubling my non-journalistic life, I will know something is wrong with it.

Yet all this said, I feel there is a good bit right with the press. The questions we raise point to the answers we can be proud of. And it was never more necessary than now to seek and be certain of those answers.

Consider our situation. World War II stirred forces and made realignments on a world scale that are hard to comprehend and harder still to measure.

We are told that America has enormous power to lead, but no one seems to have enormous will to follow. We cannot translate atomic power into jungle victory.

And on this vast scene lives modern American man, affluent beyond the imagining of Croesus, but not understanding the economics of it—in other words, not knowing where the wealth really came from or how long it will last. Mobile beyond the capacity of any previous people to move, but not really sure where he wants to go. The object of a bombardment of information more intense and more insistent than at any conceivable time in history, but always unsure of what really happened. Needing more and more to know in order to choose his way of government best, able less and less to understand.

We have a public mind, a popular consensus composed of the biggest hit songs and the highest-rated shows, the best comic strips and the latest fashions, the newest auto styles and the fattest best-sellers.

Smaller countries and older civilizations might take accepted ideas of life and, translating them into terms shared by all, make them applicable to each citizen so that every man roughly understood what his neighbor was like. But we are a huge nation, a continent wide but sometimes incredibly narrow. Our common denominators seem to get lower and more common as time passes so that the public mind, the generalities that help us understand each other, is full of trivia, impersonal and cold. It deals with masses, not with men. It doesn't enlighten, it just communicates.

The creative arts of our day are experimenting now with a way of dealing with this scene. The Picasso that hangs on my library wall is not a generation ahead of the painting we saw when I was a boy. It is a century ahead. Our music began leaping forward years ago. The drama that was once contained in neat settings and careful plots is shifting into new forms. We are testing out ways of the novel today that didn't exist in 1940.

And where these things have gone, newspapers as a creative craft must follow, but in a special course.

A newspaper is as various as the men and the community it serves. It comes into the world new each morning, yet still the same. The challenge it faces is the same as that which faces the men and women who read it—to take a stand in an embattled culture and make sense of it all. Our task is to cut through the junk in the public mind by seeking the order that underlies the clutter of small events; to winnow out of the apparent what is the real; to cede to television and radio the mere repetition of activities and to look behind the bare event for meanings.

Increasingly, those meanings are personal. A newspaper is no longer the only chronicle of events. It is a guide and an interpreter for the reader. It daily grasps the whole cultural kaleidoscope and brings it into focus in terms that will interest him, be meaningful to him—talk to him, like a human being talking to another human being.

Fifty years ago our industry fell in love with a convention of objectivity that was to lay a dead hand of pattern on our news pages and freeze us into "good form." But the reporter who writes "objectively" still selects the items he puts into the story, the editor still selects the stories that make up the page and the publisher still selects the men. And in the spaces between their several objectivities—in what they leave out—may lie the real life of our time, the real color, the grainy detail that mean the difference between the clear ring of life on the printed page and just another newspaper story.

What we should worry about more is whether we are using the freedom we have and which no bureaucrat has yet denied us, to report the way we should; whether we are organizing the material at hand so that the obvious question is not merely implied but asked outright; so that the story about an anti-welfare town manager in some New York community—the one that points up a general trend in our society through a specific man in a real setting—is not hidden in the background because the main stories of the day are dreary repetitions of previous handouts. This is the real excellence of editing.

We all speak a language of marvelous flexibility and great precision that has become tortured through the usages of haste and headline writing into a cliché form that seems comfortable because it is old but has become almost unnoticed, ugly. Maybe it is only new clichés we need. I trust not. But certainly there is a modern idiom that has largely passed the newspapers by, just as there is a grace and precision that seldom seems quite translated into their pages. It is not good enough to look at the readers and say they are happy with what they have. We are supposed to lead; we must challenge them to move ahead with us or neither of us will move at all. We will slide, as a craft, as a profession and as readers, too, into the stagnation of shopping sheets, throwaways and the junior partner of television.

The role we can play every day, if we try, is to take the whole experience of every day and shape it to involve American man. It is our job to interest him in his community and to give his ideas the excitement they should have. These are the excellences of our craft.

They are produced by men who are truly engaged in producing the poetry of everyday life. The task of poetry remains the old calling: To take the language and using the matter at hand, speak to the mind and the heart of individual men. It is the calling of newspapers also; it is their challenge. The excellence of publishers lies in recognizing this and in providing the opportunity and the goad for men of varying talents to reach out beyond their best to meet the challenge.

Hold the cards of your values away from your chest for a moment to see them clearly. Some, like loyalty and honor, have a schoolboy look about them and get praised dutifully—even automatically. Some, like taste and appreciation of what's fun in life, get neglected. Some, like involvement in life and the necessity for individual response, are actively challenged by everything around us and are in the greatest need of repair.

Then look back 100 years when this industrial society was being shaped and Matthew Arnold made it personal. The world, he said,

> Hath really neither joy, nor love, nor light,
> Nor certitude, nor peace, nor help for pain;
> And we are here as on a darkling plain
> Swept with confused alarms of struggle and flight,
> Where ignorant armies clash by night.

Is it true? Are the Mods and Rockers who fight now on Dover Beach a mockery of history, a cheap jest to show how low the truth has fallen from that cry of poetry?

No, I think that the ignorant armies have always been with us and I believe, as a passionate, personal thing, that joy and love and light exist here. Perhaps it would be hard for someone for a lifetime associated only with newspapers to recognize or then to boast that newspapers have within them the capability to write the real poetry of everyday life. Perhaps, too, I am a square in a hip world. But I think that in our present problems lies future greatness. I know that I have a newspaper reaching slowly forward along this path. I believe that together we see a profession that can accept its challenges and make them excellences.

THE SCIENTIST AS A HUMAN BEING [5]

GLENN T. SEABORG [6]

In a provocative essay entitled "Science Pauses," in the May 1965 issue of *Fortune,* Dr. Vannevar Bush remarks that "people have always held queer ideas about scientists." But with the advent of the A-bomb the attitude changed: "Now scientists are regarded as supermen." Dr. Bush then discusses the "inherent limitations of science," indicating that when it comes to the questions of free will and consciousness, it cannot prove, "or even bear evidence." So his final word to the young man: "As always he will build his own concepts, and his own loyalties. He will follow science where it leads, but will not attempt to follow where it cannot lead. And, with a pause, he will admit a faith."

With a different point of focus and emphasis, Dr. Glenn T. Seaborg, chairman of the Atomic Energy Commission, also points to the changing conception of the scientist. On the occasion of his receiving the Charles Lathrop Parsons Award of the American Chemical Society in Washington, D.C., on December 5, 1964, he reminded his audience that the scientist is no longer viewed as a "visionary eccentric." Rather, he is now seen as "a human being because he is willing to look beyond the immediate results of his scientific endeavors to their social consequences." Moreover, Dr. Seaborg notes an increasing acceptance of the scientists by the nonscientists on these terms: "They do so realizing that only by cooperative efforts . . . will we be able to achieve the higher levels of human behavior toward which we are all striving."

Dr. Seaborg's statement is another in a continuing line of important addresses by modern men of science. Regular readers of REPRESENTATIVE AMERICAN SPEECHES will recall Dr. Seaborg's Wesley Powell Lecture which appeared in the 1961-1962 edition; Loren Eiseley's "Man: The Lethal Factor," in 1962-1963; C. P. Snow's "The Moral Un-neutrality of Science," in 1960-1961; and P. B. Sears' "Science, Life, and Landscape," in 1961-1962.

I can think of few events during recent years that have given me more real pleasure and satisfaction than the American Chemical Society's notification that I was to receive the Charles

---

[5] Text furnished by Dr. Seaborg, with permission for this reprint.

[6] For biographical note, see Appendix.

Lathrop Parsons Award. For one thing it was like being told that I had done a fairly presentable job of what I had been urging other scientists to do—that is, to devote more of their thought and energies to matters of public concern. It is always good to feel that you have been able in some degree to practice what you preach. There is pleasure too in knowing you have been thought of along with such people as the original recipient of this award, the grand old man of the American Chemical Society, Charlie Parsons—not to mention James Conant, Roger Adams and George Kistiakowsky. Tonight I want to speak of scientists as people—as human beings.

Old legends die hard, but none has been more persistent than the belief that the scientist is something more, or perhaps something less, than a human being. The image of the scientist as a misguided or visionary eccentric is almost as old as Western culture. In fact, Aristophanes wrote one of his most successful comedies on this theme and spoke of the scientists of his day, certain philosophers, as dwellers in Cloud-Cuckooland. But the image of the scientist as a more or less wicked wizard is perhaps even more ancient. You will recall that the demigod Prometheus stole fire from heaven and was rewarded by his superiors for this bit of insolence by being sentenced to an eternal career as a bird-feeding station. Whether or not he was wicked depended upon whether you took sides with the gods or Prometheus's human beneficiaries.

To say the least, people have always felt some uneasiness upon being confronted with new knowledge and have been inclined to distrust the purveyors of such knowledge. The quasi-legendary figure of Dr. Faustus represents one reaction—that of awe-struck fear; the dwellers in Cloud-Cuckooland and their successors in the writings of Jonathan Swift are the products of another, more positive reaction—ridicule.

The two images vacillate in time with the successes and failures of science, with some component of each usually present in our culture. I believe most of you who have had the experience of presenting testimony to a congressional committee will agree that the picture of a scientist blissfully floating along on cloud nine has not entirely disappeared, even with the great prestige that science now enjoys. And perhaps it is a sign of good mental health on the part of the average citizen that he is still able to have some fun at our expense.

When science was young, when the distinguished amateurs of the early British scientific societies were looking into all sorts of questions, the satire directed at experimenters often became biting and remarkably detailed. Interestingly enough, some of what Swift intended for satire has turned out to be, from the viewpoint of our times, more nearly prophetic than satirical.

Still there is plenty of bite in the scenes portraying Gulliver's visit to the Grand Academy of Lagado. Here is Gulliver's account of his initial encounter with science: "The first man I saw was of a meagre aspect, with sooty hands and face, his hair and beard long, ragged, and singed in several places. His clothes, shirt, and skin were all of the same color. He had been eight years upon a project for extracting sunbeams out of cucumbers, which were to be put in phials hermetically sealed, and let out to warm the air in raw inclement summers. He told me, he did not doubt, that in eight years or more, he should be able to supply the governor's gardens with sunshine, at a reasonable rate; but he complained that his stock was low, and entreated me to give him something as an encouragement to ingenuity, especially since this had been a very dear season for cucumbers."

Times have changed a great deal. I am confident that our people working on their project of producing miniature suns by means of the controlled fusion process have better prospects than the cucumber expert of the Grand Academy; science requires substantial sums for its support in these days, and we are not alarmed when our controlled thermonuclear scientists indicate at budget time that it is going to be a "very dear season for cucumbers." The whole progress of physical science separates these men from the objects of Swift's satire. We are able to point to measurable progress in our controlled thermonuclear program, giving us ground for reasonable optimism.

"In another apartment," Gulliver says, "I was highly pleased with a projector who had found a device of ploughing the ground with hogs, to save the charge of ploughs, cattle, and labor. . . ." The idea, of course, was that the hogs in rooting around for delectable objects underground would pulverize the soil. "It is true," he adds, that "upon experiment, they found the charge and trouble very great, and they had little or no crop." Here Swift's satire proved to be a very accurate prediction. Large flocks of geese are now being used to keep cotton plantations and peppermint fields free of weeds with a considerable savings over traditional methods. In the case of the peppermint fields, however, the geese develop a taste for the young peppermint plants and have to be retired after a couple of years.

The tasks on which Swift had the chemists engaged would hardly bear repetition in the polite society of his day or our own. I will therefore leave these scenes to the sufficiently curious reader except to mention that one prospector was "at work to calcine ice into gunpowder" and that he had also completed a treatise concerning the "malleability of fire"—not very promising endeavors.

I cannot leave the Grand Academy of Lagado without recalling at least one other project which—with apologies to our colleagues in the field of machine translation, teaching machines and information processing—has a very modern ring to it. The head of this project explained to Gulliver that "everyone knew how laborious the usual method is of attaining to arts and sciences; whereas by his contrivance, the most ignorant person, at a reasonable charge, and with a little bodily labor, might write books in philosophy, poetry, politics, laws, mathematics, and theology, without the least assistance from genius or study." Gulliver says: "He then led me to the frame, about the sides whereof all his pupils stood in ranks. It was twenty feet square, placed in the middle of the room. The superficies was composed of several bits of wood, about the bigness of a die, but some larger than others. They were all linked together by slender wires. These bits of wood were covered, on every square, with paper pasted on them; and on these papers were written all the words of their language, in their several moods, tenses, and declensions; but without any order."

To make a long story short, some of the pupils by turning cranks on this machine changed the pattern of the words while others transcribed the bits and pieces of sentences that appeared. Gulliver relates that he was shown several volumes in large folio, already collected, of broken sentences, which were eventually to give the world a complete body of all arts and sciences. It may be that the researchers of the Grand Academy are still ahead of our progress in this field. However, a poet of my acquaintance tells me that one of his beatnik colleagues uses a simplified version of the Academy's composition machine. A bottle filled with scraps of paper on which words are written is shaken up by this fellow and his poems are then composed using words from the scraps of paper as these are drawn one by one from the bottle.

Swift concludes his account of Lagado and its projects by anticipating Korzybski's school of general semantics. He tells of scientists who have eschewed the use of language altogether and converse with each other by pointing to particular objects out of a collection they carry about with them for purposes of discussion. He remarks that when the universe of discourse is large the burden can get rather heavy and cumbersome. In Gulliver's opinion, however, this invention might well have been adopted "if the women, in conjunction with the vulgar and illiterate, had not threatened to raise a rebellion unless they might be allowed the liberty to speak with their tongues after the manner of their forefathers; such constant irreconcilable enemies to science are the common people!"

While, as I have admitted, the image of the scientist as an otherworldly bungler is still with us, in recent years and especially since the earthshaking advent of nuclear energy the Faustian figure has again been renewed with some potency. It is very difficult for the majority of mankind to regard those who have had a hand in the release of such an awesome power of destruction as not having some infernal motivation. The process of demonstrating to the world that the beneficial aspects of nuclear energy can in the long run outweigh its potential evil will require the devoted and patient efforts of many men over many years. We have only begun to rebuild our confidence.

Nor is nuclear energy the only cause for apprehension concerning the products of applied science. Unfortunate results from the use of some modern drugs and the deleterious effects of pesticides when improperly used have caused widespread concern. The knowledge that chemical and biological agents have been developed to refined stages of destructiveness has had a disquieting effect on many people. Even those technological applications, such as computers and automation, which without question will prove to be immensely liberating for man everywhere, have raised specters of painful economic and social dislocation. The scientist as the moving force behind a vast new array of technology must expect that he will to some extent become the focus of these anxieties, even while his status and prestige increase due to the benefits his work has achieved.

The title of a recent survey of science fiction, *New Maps of Hell*, gives the flavor of many of the stories in this burgeoning field of literature. Many of these stories deal imaginatively with the kinds of reactions, either disastrous or beneficial, that society may experience in adapting to extremes of technological advancement in the near and more remote future. But the point can now be made most forcibly that never again will the scientist appear to be a distant figure isolated from the common concerns of everyday human beings. Never again will science appear to be an esoteric philosophy pursued merely for the disinterested intellectual pleasure of a few individuals. Science is so intimately connected with all levels of our life today, from the most utilitarian technology to the highest reaches of our intellectual endeavors, that there can be no question of escaping its pervasive influence. However, it is interesting to note in this connection that Einstein's work set off a far-reaching train of reactions among philosophers even before it demonstrated its concrete potentialities in helping to provide us with a new form of energy.

Thus, while we may occasionally be able to point to seem-ingly ridiculous aberrations, the layman is likely to feel uncertain that even the wildest may not turn up something important. Science has demonstrated its potency over and over again, and as a result we have to put ourselves in a special frame of mind to find the experiments conducted at the Grand Academy of Lagado anything like as humorous as they seemed to Swift's contempo-raries.

These then are the traditional stereotypes, and though they are waning we must admit that, since scientists include very nearly the whole range of traits found in the human species, there are elements of truth in both of our stock character versions of the scientist. The scientist as the visionary bungler stubbing his toe over the most obvious facts of life certainly has his coun-terpart in everyday experience. Indeed the very fact of asking a lot of questions is sure to produce a lot of wrong answers. But it is the virtue of science over the long run to put these wrong answers to the test of reality and relegate them to the junk heap of human experience.

Ordinarily it is only among the unenlightened that the more extreme errors continue their precarious day-to-day existence. Naturally there are exceptions to this rule. Even well into this century I have been told there was a professional man—the pro-fession to remain anonymous—who explained malaria as an illness that arises from eating cornbread. Among scientists, of course, there will continue to be those worthy of the highest honors accorded them and the exceptional few who help to perpetuate the image of the theoretical bungler. I have heard one story of an investigator, one of our contemporaries, who was studying the growth rate effects of planting Irish potatoes during different phases of the moon. Perhaps by now he has succeeded in establishing a correlation.

And the scientist is human in other respects, as many a government and university administrator has discovered when trying to economize at the expense of a scientist's favorite project. His attachment to the things that are peculiarly his own is just as strong as the painter's identification with his canvas or the novelist's feelings for the characters coming to life under his pen. He is human and selfish, at least to that extent.

Those familiar with the history of science are aware also that the scientist can be very human on questions concerning the priority of discoveries. There may not have been quite so many words expended on the famous Newton-Leibniz controversy as have been devoted to the authorship of Shakespeare's plays, but the human feelings involved were unmistakably intense. Today perhaps, with our emphasis on group research in large organizations, we are more inclined to recognize the likelihood of simultaneous advances and be more lenient with claims and counterclaims. Nevertheless there is still a healthy spirit of competition.

The image of the scientist as a visionary eccentric has faded away and the wicked wizard picture has been revived only now and then by the spectacular potency of modern science. For the most part, the scientist tends to look more and more like the rest of the population. His numbers are increasing as science prospers and its benefits spread to the far corners of the earth.

Most of us would be hurt and disappointed, I think, if we could easily be distinguished from the lawyer, the business executive, a professor of the humanities, or a successful football coach. The image of the scientist has in fact begun to assume ordinary human proportions. To the extent that this image looms at all larger than life, it is due to the increasing involvement of the scientific community in the affairs of state and industry. Along with this involvement and a correspondingly rapid growth in the number of people choosing science as a career, there has been a major escalation of the scientist in the public's esteem. The University of Chicago's National Opinion Research Center issued recently a draft report entitled "Occupational Prestige in the United States: 1925-1962." This report lists the first nine occupations ranked according to prestige as follows: supreme court justice, physician, nuclear physicist, scientist, government scientist, state governor, cabinet member in the Federal Government, college professor, and United States representative in Congress.

A similar study was made in 1947 and the major difference between these two studies was a rise in the prestige of scientists.

The most remarkable change was in the status accorded to nuclear physicists, apparently a somewhat delayed reaction to events during World War II. While the studies in each case showed that only a very small proportion, from 2 to 3 per cent, of the respondents could describe the duties of a nuclear scientist, there was undoubtedly a realization that this scientist was the man responsible for nuclear weapons. It may be also that the nuclear scientist has become the most articulate representative of the scientific community.

At any rate, the post-World War II years have seen not only a change in the public image of the scientist, but an equally profound change in the scientist's attitude toward himself and his work. The soul-searching among scientists of the Manhattan Project, as that endeavor reached its culmination, is too well evidenced in subsequent events to need retelling. There is hardly a one of the major contributors to the project who has not felt the need to participate in developing public policy with regard to the control of nuclear energy in its military and peaceful uses. There has been a marked willingness of scientists in recent years to enter the public service, sometimes even at a considerable personal sacrifice.

What is now emerging, I believe, is an era in which the scientist will achieve increasing stature as a human being because he is willing to look beyond the immediate results of his scientific endeavors to their social consequences. He recognizes that even though he cannot presume to advise mankind with finality on the values that are most acceptable for our world, at least he may be able to help point out the probable consequences of pursuing alternative courses according to one or another set of values. And he realizes that he, in common with men generally, will be deeply affected by the course that is chosen.

I believe further that nonscientists are coming to accept the scientist and his science on these terms. They do so realizing that only by cooperative efforts involving scientist and layman, deeply committed to the need for resolving the extremely complex problems we face in this age, will we be able to achieve the higher levels of human behavior toward which we are all striving.

THE GOSPEL OF INSECURITY [7]

SAMUEL H. MILLER [8]

American oratorical history records many sermons among its most distinctive contributions. Anthologies of speeches are likely to include works by Jonathan Edwards, Henry Ward Beecher, Phillips Brooks, Theodore Parker—to mention but a few—and more recently, Harry Emerson Fosdick, Robert McCracken, Eugene Carson Blake, Gerald Kennedy—again to mention but a few.

In recent months, the role of the clergy in the civil rights movement has, of course, focused attention on many socially oriented sermons. And everyone recalls the publicity attending the address by the Very Reverend Francis B. Sayre, Jr., in Washington Cathedral on September 13, 1964, in which he deplored the choice confronting the voters in the last presidential campaign. But many excellent sermons fail to get a wide audience, and hence escape the compiler's notice. They have to compete with countless other sermons given on the same day, and in countless places. Unless they contain a dramatic item which captures the attention of the press, they probably will end up in the preacher's file, never again to see the light of day. (Periodically, one should add, the entire function of the sermon in religious expression is questioned. See, for example, Alexander Graubart's "Are Sermons Necessary?" in *The Reconstructionist*, 29:24-26, April 1963; and Arthur Bronstein's reply "In Defense of Sermons," in *Essays in Honor of Walter Plaut*.)

The editor believes the sermon below deserves wide reading. It was given by Dr. Samuel H. Miller, Dean of the Harvard Divinity School, in the Pomona College Chapel, Claremont, California, on November 8, 1964. Author of many books and an active minister ever since he was ordained in 1923, Dean Miller thoughtfully inquires "whether we can stretch ourselves, our humanity, to match the magnitude of our technological achievement." And he pleads for "a new kind of man"—one with "larger vision, a more flexible will, a vaster compassion, a keener perception, a saner judgment, a surer sense of values."

And a ruler asked him, "Good Teacher, what shall I do to inherit eternal life?" And Jesus said to him, "Why do you call me good? No one is good but God alone.

[7] Text furnished by Dean Miller, with permission for this reprint.
[8] For biographical note, see Appendix.

You know the commandments: 'Do not commit adul-
tery, Do not kill, Do not steal, Do not bear false witness,
Honor your father and mother.'" And he said, "All
these I have observed from my youth." And when Jesus
heard it, he said to him, "One thing you still lack. Sell
all that you have and distribute to the poor, and you will
have treasure in heaven; and come, follow me." But
when he heard this he became sad, for he was very rich.
Jesus looking at him said, "How hard it is for those who
have riches to enter the kingdom of God!"

—*Luke*, 18:18-24

This interview must have been bewildering for the rich young
ruler. He was obviously a rather self-assured young man, who
thought of himself as good, for had he not "kept the law from his
youth up." Given such an assumption, his head must have spun
to have heard Jesus' quick rejoinder to his courteous address:
"Why do you call me good?" Had he not realized that there are
all kinds of goodness, that some kinds are not worth much, and
indeed some we know are simply good for nothing. There is a
goodness which is only skin deep; a goodness displayed for the
sake of reputation; a goodness that confuses respectability with
righteousness; a goodness that keeps the law but breaks the spirit;
a goodness that grows vain and in its vanity becomes cruel and
condescending; a goodness that plays it safe behind every moral-
ism and avoids inconvenience as if it were the plague; a goodness
that is good within the patterns of the past but with no eye for
the present evil; a goodness that clings to distant benevolences
but is blind to shrieking injustice or crucifixions near at hand.
Goodness is as corruptible as anything else. Once it is corrupted,
it tends to appear in its most impeccable assumptions.

But deeper than that, the rich young ruler must have been
rudely shocked when he certified his own righteousness by saying
he had kept the law from his youth up. He had obeyed his
parents, conformed to the norms of his community, fulfilled the

expectations of his society—in short, his reputation was beyond question. And in the bargain, God in his good pleasure had given him great wealth. The picture is complete, indeed just about perfect. Yet abruptly, Jesus replies in a short perceptive sentence which is like a lance leveled at the man. "One thing you still lack!" What could such a man lack—he had youth, a good character, a fine reputation, and wealth as well. "One thing!" What could it be?

If one is to pierce beyond the bald and shattering admonition of the Lord to sell everything and give it to the poor, one can see what the young man lacks—it is insecurity. There comes a time when a man, to be a man, must move beyond safety, beyond the easy conformities, beyond self-assurance, into the turmoil and terror of life lived heroically. If a man wants eternal life, it is to be found only at a risk, only where one pushes out into deep water. Insecurity is the name of the Christian's daring, of his faith, and ultimately of his peace in God.

Now let us not hide from the truth—you and I are living in a very insecure world. It is filled with a frightening amount of change. It is not the kind of change known a generation ago that happened once in a lifetime, but the kind that changes the earth with each step we take. Each day the world changes. Changes in business, changes in styles, changes in education, changes in morals, changes in church, changes in science. As the Angel Gabriel says in *Green Pastures*, "Everything nailed down is coming loose."

Not only is the world changing but some of the change has a massiveness about it which arouses our anxiety. For instance, it has taken the last 1,500 years to double the population of the world, but it will double again in the next fifty years, that is, in the lifetime of some who are sitting here. Moreover while this is going on, our remarkable genius in technology is managing at the moment, if we are to believe Luther Hodges, to diminish jobs in the United States by automation at the rate of 40,000 weekly! Think of what a squeeze that makes on employment, or put personally, where will our children look for jobs. Add to this dilemma the fact that in the last ten years over 800 million people have risen from primitive rural conditions and colonial subjection to industrial development and political independence. Now in this seething and jostling world, we stand with the atom bomb in our nervous, unsteady hands—destructive power enough to kill 400 million people in one hour. Doubtless that number has been increased in the last year. An insecure world indeed!

It is upsetting, disturbing, threatening! It makes for restlessness, and anxiety, and irresponsibility. Every part of society is on the move and no one stays anywhere long enough to make a stable community. Things fall apart, including the family. Traditions disappear, ideals evaporate, religion itself appears obsolete. Everywhere, whether we like the looks of it, or the feel of it, things change at a perilous pace. Insecurity belongs to this age and we cannot escape it.

Yet to be sure people will try to avoid it. They will even insist it isn't there. They will play games with it, blame it on government, or the Russians; they will seek to avoid it by running in all directions, into all kinds of escapes: gambling, paranoid politics, establishing little Shangri-Las, watching the TV, getting ensconced in some kind of a cozy cell group where they can be tranquilized. Even the church can be misused this way. For in a world of pervasive insecurity either we can react in fear and retreat to some false safety; or we can meet the challenge with faith and advance to the next stage of human destiny. The first question is whether we have the courage to share in a larger reality than that of our accustomed habit. Take for instance just the sheer size of our world. Technologically we have fabricated a web of connections so that it is now one world. We do not have to play God to make it one world. We have done that—with radio communication, with air transportation, with industrial production, and commercial markets. It is one world whether we like it or not; so much one, that what happens in Vietnam or the Congo or Moscow may decide the life and death of your sons and daughters. But having made it technologically one world, we still do not have the emotional or imaginative strength to sustain its unity morally. The fabric of speed and radio which holds everybody close together also makes it easy for suspicion or hostility or stupidity to explode the entire business in a few seconds.

The question that must be inevitably asked is whether we can stretch ourselves, our humanity to match the magnitude of our technological achievement. Put into a simple and very direct question it becomes "How wide is the circle of your imagination and compassion? How far does the hospitality of your mind and heart extend in this technologically united world? Do you push your limits only as far as the bounds of the white race—but cannot include the Negro, or the Oriental? Are you religiously unable to see or feel beyond the narrow pigeon hole of the Protestants—or can you engage in human and humane dialogue with Catholics, or Muslims or Buddhists? How large a portion of the world you have united by your science and your industry, do you support with your heart, with your good will?"

Make no mistake. God is making a new world. Larger, faster, with greater power, filled with risk and danger as every world has been—and each of us is being weighed in the balance. We are being judged. Are we fit for this new world of insecurity, or are we afraid of it? Are we debits or credits?

It is obvious in the second place that we shall not easily match the magnitude of the world's need unless we are inwardly transformed. Nineteenth century men will not solve the twentieth century problem. Too many of us are proud of driving the latest model car, insist on the most dazzling plumbing and gadgets in our homes, only to manifest a hopelessly obsolete form of Victorian morals or an utterly defunct kind of pious sentimentality. The strain of the modern world on our religion and ethics is unmeasurable, but if our religion and ethics continue to be little more than our pride in what our forefathers did in solving their problems rather than the bold and decisive action necessary to confront the larger issues of our own day, then we deserve little respect. Everything in our world demands a larger dimension of conscience, a fresh evaluation of powers and principalities, a deepening of the soul, a wider breadth of hospitality, a new sense of steadiness and poise—in short, the world demands, and must have, a new kind of man. He must transcend the patterns we know, and have honored. He must have a larger vision, a more flexible will, a vaster compassion, a keener perception, a saner judgment, a surer sense of values. He must be less suspicious, less fanatic, less frenzied, less credulous, less manipulatable. He needs more inner resources, more imagination, more character, more skepticism in some directions and more faith in others.

After the Second World War, a nasty little novel called *The Tin Drum* was written by Günter Grass and achieved best-seller fame. It was about a boy who decided at three years of age that he was never going to grow up. There are countless people in our world who have decided, at one time or another, that they were not going to grow up—at least no further. They had their little drum, their favorite tantrums, and they made out very well by staying as they were. As someone has said, in this kind of a world we only need to fear the small scale individual. His very little-ness, his shriveled fears and base denial of insecurity, will bring the larger world down around our heads. He wants everything his own size.

Ultimately of course, this means that such a world of stresses and strains, of speed and incessant change, of vast diversities and uncomfortable differences, can only be sustained by new syntheses of thought. This is the way civilization has advanced. To each complexity of heritage, a new age adds its new contribution of power and insight. It was Augustine who wove together the strong strands of Biblical religion, Roman law, and Greek philosophy which provided us with a culture for a thousand years. Our agony, stretching over the last three centuries, is the travail of adding the new factors of science and industry to the old traditions. Here in the university, by accident and by deliberation, there are many opportunities to work on the necessary syntheses by which a new world can be structured in a beauty and order we have never known before.

As often as I listen to a symphonic orchestra I am stirred by the mystery of the event. Think of it, here are a hundred men, each of whom has spent a lifetime in a passionate and consuming effort to learn his particular instrument. From early childhood, through youth and manhood, through all the anguish of our mortal dust, in loneliness, heartache, and ecstasy, despite great sorrows and minor distractions and world catastrophes, each man pours his very life into skillful fingertips, or sensitive lips, or sure hearing, until every nuance, every subtlety, every insubstantial quaver can be communicated by his violin or horn, or flute, or harp, or saxophone. Then they assemble, not to hear each other's solos, but to play together what they cannot play apart—a symphony. The souls of a hundred men, the mortal life with all its color and drama, its faith and fears—all flow into the symphony. And it hangs for a moment in the air, laving our spirits with its transfiguring beauty. It redeems us, lifts us beyond ourselves; it glorifies our common humanity.

Is there no way, in a world so magnificently empowered as our own, so magically interrelated, so burgeoning in its startling surprises, its human concern, its lively arts, to redeem us from our littleness and to lift us into the symphony of God's new creation?

THE RESTLESS GENERATION AND UNDERGRADUATE EDUCATION [9]

Robert J. Wert [10]

Student unrest at colleges and universities during the past two years has been front page copy. Reminiscent of the activities of the 1930's, it appeared, however, to have new dimensions, both in direction and in intensity. At a few institutions, notably the University of California at Berkeley, the events constituted, in the opinion of Seymour M. Lipset and Paul Seabury, "a small-scale but genuine revolution."

Student dissatisfactions—shared indeed by many faculty members as well—were varied and complex. The bigness and impersonality of some institutions contribute to the students' sense of anonymity, purposelessness, and alienation. Their insistence upon having a more active part in administrative policies, of having more to say about their education and the context in which it is offered—this, too, is critical. But more important still is the rather sudden emergence of a new attitude: the recognition that a strong student movement, politically and socially oriented, can have influence—much influence—on community and national action. The new movement bears aspects of a moral crusade.

At an honors convocation on April 26, 1965, at the California State College at Los Angeles, Dr. Robert J. Wert examined the changes in student aspirations, the drive for student "rights," and the influence of increased graduate enrollments on undergraduate instruction. Vice Provost and Dean cf Undergraduate Instruction at Stanford University, Dr. Wert speaks both as an administrator and teacher. In response to his own question, "How shall decisions be made about the future directions of American colleges and by whom?" he allowed that crises in administration will doubtless develop during the next decade. Saying that the future of the country rests upon the excellence of our colleges and universities, he concluded that

> students, faculty members, administrators, trustees, alumni, and the general public must work cooperatively, moderately and constructively to understand our colleges and help them move successfully through what will certainly be a period of trauma, travail and excitement.

Significantly, Dr. Wert puts the students at the head of his list of interested parties.

[9] Text furnished by Barbara M. Svenson, secretary to Dr. Wert, with permission for this reprint.

[10] For biographical note, see Appendix.

A few years ago reporters cringed when they were assigned the dull and boring job of covering educational topics for their newspapers. Five years ago, when California's Coordinating Council for Higher Education was established, the metropolitan newspapers of Los Angeles and San Francisco assigned reporters to the unenviable task of covering the monthly meetings of the Council. The reporters were ingenious, as reporters must be, and managed to write a few pieces which eventually saw their way into print. The stories were perhaps properly placed in the newspapers; they were located in the last section—someplace between the obituaries and the want ads. Times have changed. The president of a well-known college now has as much news value as a prominent rock-and-roll singer or a not-quite-topflight movie star. Education editors on the newspapers are surprised to find themselves nearly as important as society editors and able to command nearly as much space as police beat reporters. It is commonplace now for those of us at Stanford to expect monthly visits, at least, from the very competent education editor of the Los Angeles *Times*, Bill Trombley. *Time, Newsweek,* and even the *Wall Street Journal,* want educators' opinions on everything ranging from anthropology to zoology. Even the Coordinating Council actions hit the front page.

Newspapers and magazines, with all of their faults, develop a sensitivity to what is exciting and to what is timely. Higher education, colleges and universities, are everybody's business (and everybody considers himself an expert on colleges and education because we've all had some of it). Nearly four million American teenagers will celebrate their eighteenth birthday this year. College enrollment, which has been nearly five million this year, is expected to approach six million next year. Demand for entrance to college in our state has, for the first time, outstripped the availability of places in college. Institutions like California State College at Los Angeles now face the unpleasant task of turning away qualified students.

While more students go to college every year, and college becomes nearly as necessary for students as high school has been in the past, sit-ins and demonstrations at Berkeley, picket lines at Yale, marijuana at Cornell, and manifest student unrest at an increasing number of colleges all over the nation force us to wonder what is going on, what is different, or, perhaps, what is wrong, with American higher education.

It is my view that America's colleges and universities face a new situation—one which is unparalleled in their 300-year history. It has the following main causes: first, a significant change in the number, composition, and aspirations of college students; second, a rising tide of interest in student "rights," student "academic freedom," student "autonomy," and student "activism," particularly in the political and social arenas; and third, a rapidly rising number of graduate students and an increased emphasis on graduate work and research.

This evening I should like to analyze each of these three points and I will conclude by examining what seems to be the fundamental question before American higher education: How shall decisions be made about the future directions of American colleges and by whom?

Ever since World War II, and certainly during the last five years, colleges have been struggling to adapt themselves to different types of students than they had seen before. The present students have lived only during prosperity and do not remember World War II. President Hoover, prohibition, depression, NRA, President Roosevelt, and even Winston Churchill, who has lived during their time, are shadows to them—real, yet unreal. Their war is in Vietnam, their world is characterized by the overpowering threat of devastation from hydrogen bombs, the incessant Cold War, amazing technological changes, the culminating drive for civil rights, and the development of so many new nations that even experts on world affairs can no longer recite the names of them. Their world has shrunk so rapidly that they find it easy to identify closely with people in India, Israel, Africa, or Japan.

Moreover, the present student generation has been raised differently. By comparison with the past, their parents have been permissive, there are more broken families, and families move increasingly from place to place. The influence of psychologists and psychiatrists, increased freedom of expression in the public schools, and the pervasive intrusion of television have radically altered the experiences of youngsters. With a newly-found freedom, they have observed the adult world as it engages in a sometimes chaotic and frustrating exploration to discover significant and meaningful personal values. Their parents' generation has been involved with atonal music, abstract—and now pop—art, a literature of self-expression which sometimes borders on nihilism, and philosophies which, when understandable at all, exalt the individual, his inner beliefs, and his acts beyond everything else.

Students do not think much of the legacy which has been left them, nor do they prize so-called "experience" or "common sense." Mario Savio, the leader of the FSM movement at Berkeley, echoed the thoughts of many students when he said that students distrust everybody over age 30. Meanwhile, thanks to major improvements in high schools, present college students are far better prepared academically than any previous generation. In addition, they are more sophisticated, more traveled, more idealistic, and, I think, vastly more interesting than students used to be. (I should add that they are also more time-consuming for faculty and college administrators.)

Some students—and this so far is a small minority—have decided that reading, discussion, and learning are not enough. They want direct experience with the "real" world, with important problems. Some seek to remake the world to conform to their image of what it should be. They travel to Mississippi, picket Federal buildings, tutor underprivileged children, join the Peace Corps, engage actively in politics, and attempt to reform society's various institutions—including colleges.

Another thing we should note about present students is that they have labored under considerable pressure to do well in school, to get good grades, to get into college, and that this pressure begins even in the elementary schools. When they finally get to college, the pressure continues and the competition mounts.

Then they worry about whether they will be admitted to the best graduate and professional schools, and over half of them now in college will go on for graduate work. The pressure to obtain good grades has turned them into young Scrooges; they consider grades to be the basic currency of the college. These students are the serious generation, as well as the restless generation.

During the last ten years or more, many of us working in colleges have been willing participants in the nationwide crusade to improve the intellectual environment of high schools. It is interesting to notice that critical attention to the high school curriculum began when the post-World War II babies started to inundate the high schools. That same large group now storms the college gates. My guess is that the counterparts of Rickover, Conant, Bestor, and the other critics of the high school, will now aim and fire at the colleges. Open season on higher education is about to begin. Professors and college presidents should polish their bulletproof vests and prepare to defend themselves from all sides.

To come to my second point, the next change confronting the colleges is the growing student drive for self-determination and autonomy. Historically, this is a relatively new concept. College faculties and college presidents heretofore have tended to be high-handed, if not obstreperous, in dealing with students. But things seem to be changing. The American Civil Liberties Union, the National Student Association, the American Association of University Professors, the newly-formed Students for a Democratic Society, and recent critics of the colleges such as Paul Goodman, have all asserted that, like other Americans, students have certain "inalienable rights." The definitions of these rights vary. The ACLU is particularly concerned with legal due process for students involved in disciplinary hearings on college campuses. The National Student Association has this interest, but along with the AAUP, extends it to rights of students to invite controversial speakers to campuses, rights of free speech to students, and rights for student participation in decisions within colleges and universities.

While all of this may seem new in the United States, it is not new in other countries. Many students are aware of the fact that the earliest university in the Western world, the University of Bologna, in Italy, was organized and controlled by students in the eleventh century. They realize that the influence of the University of Bologna extended into modern times in such diverse areas of the world as Latin America, India, and Japan, where students not only have a powerful voice in university affairs, but also in national politics. Student demonstrations and riots are commonplace in these countries. It wasn't long ago when student demonstrations in Japan were a sufficient threat to force President Eisenhower to cancel a proposed trip. The more activist American students know that students in other countries have exerted powerful influences. Their own experiences with the FSM movement at the University of California at Berkeley, the Student Non-Violent Coordinating Committee in the South, and the recent Students for a Democratic Society march on Washington to protest the war in Vietnam, demonstrate that American students, if properly organized, can be a potent social and political force. FSM-type movements are sprouting on campuses all over the United States. We are witnessing a nationwide phenomenon which will continue and which may change both our educational and political processes. Powerful elements of the right, the left, and the center will ultimately be involved. A principal contest for the minds of students will be waged in the colleges. It will be serious, for keeps, and for high stakes. Soon the students now in high school and college will control the vote.

So far, most of the students' thunder has come from the left, and much of the adult thunder has come from the right. Adult conservatives, like members of the John Birch Society, continue, as they have in the past, to attack the way economics, particularly, and social sciences, in general, are taught in the colleges. So far, they do not seem to realize that the battle has shifted, that their war has escalated beyond the limited boundaries of classical versus Keynesian economics. The Port Huron Statement of the left-wing Students for a Democratic Society, and the existence of chapters of that Society on campuses all over the country, point to the new conflict and the new battleground. The Port Huron Statement, which has been widely circulated, concludes by asserting:

> From its schools and colleges across the nation, a militant left might awaken its allies, and by beginning the process toward peace, civil rights, and labor struggles, reinsert theory and idealism where too often reign confusion and political barter; it has shown its actuality in the South, and in the reform movement of the North. . . .

> To turn these possibilities into realities will involve national efforts at university reform by an alliance of students and faculty. They must wrest control of the educational process from the administrative bureaucracy. They must make fraternal and functional contact with allies in labor, civil rights, and other liberal forces outside the campus. They must import major public issues into the curriculum—research and teaching on problems of war and peace is an outstanding example. They must make debate and controversy, not dull pedantic cant, the common style for educational life. They must consciously build a base for their assault upon the loci of power.

During the last year, leadership among the students at Berkeley and at some other colleges has been taken over by left-wing reformers. The moderates and conservatives have been strangely silent, and either inactive or ineffective. In a prophetic passage in his brilliant book, *The Uses of a University*, Clark Kerr described the consequences of extremists' control of the university: "To make the multiversity work really effectively, the moderates need to be in control of each power center and there needs to be an attitude of tolerance between and among the power centers, with few territorial ambitions. When the extremists get in control of the students, the faculty, or the trustees with class warfare concepts, then the 'delicate balance of interests' becomes an actual war."

My third point is that the rise of graduate student enrollment is changing the face of the university. Up to the end of World War II, universities like Berkeley and Stanford concentrated most of their attention upon the education of undergraduates. These institutions, and others like them, have responded magnificently during the last twenty years to the country's desperate need for more college teachers, for more highly trained engineers and scientists, and for research important not only to individual faculty members, but to the health, welfare, and strength of the country. Research and graduate instruction inevitably take a great deal of faculty time. But undergraduates are beginning to demand equal attention. They decry the depersonalization which exists on many campuses; they cringe at the "manpower" approach to education which perceives students as statistics in a national game of the production of engineers, or mathematicians, or whatever. Moreover, they search for something with which to identify, and the search is not easy in a large university. In former years, undergraduate students could envelop themselves in an association with their college. Having but one life to give for good old Yale was once an understandable sentiment. The college student of yesteryear knew most of his fellow students and knew his instructors. A genuine sense of community existed and what was important to one was, in a sense, important to all. Going to college was a highly personal experience and the choice of college had lasting effects. The graduate of a college was "molded" by his experience. The difference between a Harvard graduate and a Yale graduate was easily perceptible to the trained eye. A graduate of Smith and a graduate of Vassar were noticeably different. By contrast, the undergraduate in a university of 20,000 or 30,000 students can be hopelessly and tragically lost. When he enters college at about 18, he is neither quite an adolescent nor quite an adult. He is searching for an identity of his own, to find out what kind of person he is, to see how he compares with others, and to establish his own philosophy of life. He wants desperately to be a participant in a community which cares about him. He believes that faculty members should worry at least as much about him as about the research projects they are pursuing with the aid of money from the Federal Government. He scorns the rules and regulations of the IBM machine type university, but at the same time is tortuously looking for help in forming his own moral code.

Undergraduate students are now demanding that they receive a fair share of the university's effort. They are insisting that universities reorganize themselves so that students will no longer feel isolated or alienated from the university community. Many of them thirst for an education which is more personal than can be achieved in large lectures, by television, or by teaching machines. Faculty members at colleges all over the country are beginning to show concern for the students' criticisms. Small colleges, large colleges, universities, and multiversities are beginning to stir themselves into thought and action. But faculty machinery grinds slowly and faculties are loath to change established procedures. The students are impatient. If normal college decision-making processes are too slow and cumbersome, they will resort to quick and direct action as they have at Berkeley and many other colleges across the country. Students are determined to improve their educational possibilities now, while they are still in college. They feel harried and restless.

So far, we have observed that our colleges and universities face awesome challenges in attempting to educate a heretofore unimaginable number of undergraduate students, some of whom are openly dissatisfied with their college experience. At the same time, in response to pressing national needs, faculty members spend more and more time on their research and the instruction of their graduate students. While students are concerned about the quality of their education, they realize that, if properly organized, they can exert pressure and influence, not only on educational matters, but in the political arena as well.

This brings us to our final question: How shall decisions be made about the future directions of American colleges and by whom?

Heretofore, the battle for power within universities has been waged between faculty members, administrators, and boards of trustees. Early in the history of our colleges, there were no particular problems in decision-making because the number of faculty members was so small. The president of the college was generally considered to be "first among equals," and his authority posed no threat to his colleagues on the faculty. During the early part of the nineteenth century, however, colleges had become larger and a few faculty members had experienced the greater freedom accorded the faculty in the great German universities of that period. In 1825, at Harvard, for example, a large number of the faculty combined to assert that only members of the faculty had the right to membership in the Harvard Corporation, which, in that institution, is the equivalent of a Board of Trustees. The faculty lost the argument, but in losing, won a delegation of considerable authority over the curriculum and teaching practices. Later in the nineteenth century, and early in the twentieth century, strong college presidents, like Charles W. Eliot at Harvard, Henry Tappan at Michigan, David Starr Jordan at Stanford, and Charles Rainey Harper at the University of Chicago, ran their institutions much like the tycoons of the same period were running their business enterprises. At this time, many college presidents could accurately be described as "autocrats," benevolent or otherwise. They could and did refer to the college as "my college," the faculty as "my faculty," and the trustees as "my board." Finally, some of these autocrats overstepped and interfered unduly with the activities of faculty members, and occasionally even fired them without sufficient cause. The beginning of the end of the tycoon phase of university management came with the formation of the American Association of University Professors in 1915. The AAUP became an association of professionals who were teachers in American colleges. The AAUP resembled the associations of lawyers and physicians —the American Bar Association and the American Medical Association. From its beginning until now, the AAUP has concentrated its efforts on the protection of the academic freedom of its members and their concomitant rights of tenure. In addition, the AAUP has been a watchdog barking loudly at misuses of power by college administrators.

Savage attacks by faculty members on the power and prerogatives of administrators and trustees also characterized the early part of the twentieth century. These critics expressed the view that colleges and universities were controlled and dominated by the representatives of big business. Upton Sinclair, for example, in his book, *The Goose Step,* analyzed the membership of boards of trustees of some of the more noted colleges in the country. He asserted that trustees were predominantly corporation executives or corporation lawyers. He observed that many of the college trustees were directors of large corporations and that often trustees of the same college were directors of the same corporation. Finally, he argued vehemently that Columbia University was controlled by the J. P. Morgan interests, that the University of Chicago was dominated by the Rockefellers, that Stanford was dominated by the western railroad interests, and so on. Sinclair and Thorstein Veblen, the great economist, urged faculty members to take over control of college administration and abolish administrators and trustees. They deplored what they termed big business intervention in the scholarly life, and saw as the only solution control from within the institution by the faculty.

It did not occur to the early critics of the colleges to think of students as possible participants in decision-making. Faculty members then simply did not consider students as equal participants in the community of scholars, nor as sophisticated enough to participate in anything except listening to what the faculty had to teach.

It is a wholly novel and recent phenomenon that critics of the colleges argue that students have a right to participate in college decisions which affect them and to share decision-making power with the faculty. In his recent, widely-read book, *The Community of Scholars,* Paul Goodman suggests the formation of many new colleges where perhaps five to ten faculty members, and one hundred students, could jointly explore and learn without outside interference from any source. Goodman's criticism is, in many respects, trenchant and to the point, although I believe his solutions are Utopian, impractical, and naïve considering the number of students who must be educated. His main innovation, and in a sense his main value, is that he dramatically calls attention to the student and the student's part in the learning process. Goodman understandably has become the Pied Piper to many students. He also has become a gadfly biting at the tough hides of college administrators and at the more tender hides of college trustees. Who shall control universities? No one knows, but many care. We are sure that the contest for control will be waged internally between students, faculty, administrators, and trustees, and externally by many factions attempting to gain control of universities to advance their particular social or political beliefs. Colleges in many ways are the most democratic, yet anarchical, institutions in society. They are democratic because many persons share participation in decisions which affect them. They are anarchical because they have few regulations and little hierarchy. They try to be informal; they try to be a genuine association of scholars. They require, as Kerr has suggested, a consensus of the moderates in order to function effectively. Universities have successfully countered dangerous assaults from within and without since they were first founded in the eleventh century. They will continue to do so.

In conclusion, I believe that many of us are going to be disturbed about various crises in colleges and universities during the next decade. The college has become one of society's most valued and essential institutions. As such, it should be criticized. As such, it will be attacked. I urge that each of us, in his own way, should learn more about the aims and functions of colleges so that we can better understand what they do and how well they do it. The future of this state and of our country rests squarely upon the character and quality of our colleges and universities. If this is true, students, faculty members, administrators, trustees, alumni, and the general public must work cooperatively, moderately and constructively to understand our colleges and help them move successfully through what will certainly be a period of trauma, travail and excitement.

EDUCATION AND PUBLIC POLICY [11]

J. W. FULBRIGHT [12]

Slightly more than a year ago, Senator J. W. Fulbright of Arkansas delivered a foreign policy speech entitled "Old Myths and New Realities" before the United States Senate. His audience was small, suggesting, perhaps, the accuracy of Tristram Coffin's remark that the senators "rarely read a Fulbright speech until they discover in the next morning's Washington *Post* that it has caused a world sensation." His address of March 25, 1964, almost did that. Both at home and abroad reactions to the statement poured in for weeks. And the dialogue on the attitudes and values he explored continues. Students who have not yet read the text can find it in many sources, including REPRESENTATIVE AMERICAN SPEECHES for 1963-1964.

The address reprinted below is less dramatic than last year's entry. But it is a stimulating, provocative report. Ranging far beyond the conventional treatment of Federal assistance to the school system, it traces many of the relationships between political action—both domestic and foreign—and educational practices in the United States. This is the sort of theme which the speaker is eminently well prepared to develop. He is a former professor of law and president of the University of Arkansas, and chairman of the powerful Senate Foreign Relations Committee.

"Education and Public Policy" was delivered on January 16, 1965, before the National Association of Secondary School Principals, meeting at Miami Beach, Florida.

A note of incidental interest: To the editor's knowledge, Senator Fulbright is the only speaker to appear in this series whose name has entered the language. *Webster's New International Dictionary,* Third Edition, includes "Fulbright," meaning a scholarship grant.

George Bernard Shaw wrote that "we have no more right to consume happiness without producing it than to consume wealth without producing it." In our affluent society we are blessed with both continually rising production and continually rising consumption of material wealth. At the same time, we are

[11] Text furnished by Senator Fulbright, with permission for this reprint.
[12] For biographical note, see Appendix.

not keeping pace in the production of those human resources that make for quality and creativity in our lives. In these areas—the vital areas of the public happiness—we have begun to live off our intellectual capital, trying to consume more happiness than our efforts are producing.

I do not suggest that the levels of taste and intellect and education are declining in America. On the contrary, they are rising impressively. Throughout the country more Americans are receiving better education than ever and more of our citizens are coming into contact with good books, good music and good art, good theater and good films than ever before. We are providing substantially increased funds for education, especially higher education, and are at last beginning to pay our teachers better if not yet adequate salaries. As one well-known professor has put it, we have come at last to understand that the edification of the spirit need not be accompanied by the mortification of the flesh.

The problem, and the paradox, is that the rise in the standards of quality and creativity in our private life—standards which inevitably are reflected in our public life—is impressive but not yet adequate to our needs. At a time when material affluence is liberating millions of people for the pursuit of individual excellence, and when technological progress requires greater wisdom and greater intellect in public life than have ever been required before, we are not keeping pace. The central problem is that while our standards of quality and creativity are rising, our need for these is increasing even faster, and a potentially dangerous gap has opened between our production and consumption of human excellence.

The Federal Government, under Presidents Kennedy and Johnson, has become well aware of the widening "education gap." Over the past four years the Federal Government has conducted an extensive and largely successful campaign to awaken public and congressional opinion to the crisis in education and to the need for a national program to deal with it. In 1964 the Congress, which has so often tried and so often failed to act effectively in this field, adopted extensive legislation for the support of education, especially higher education. At present the prospects are bright for the enactment by Congress of a broad program of assistance to primary and secondary education along the lines proposed by President Johnson in his State of the Union address and in the special message on education which he sent to the Congress four days ago.

There have been regrettable delays in the initiation of a national program for expanding the scope and improving the quality of public education. These delays have been caused by controversies that have little to do with education itself—controversies relating to race relations, to church-state relations, and to relations between the state and Federal Governments. Unfortunately it has been the fate of education—like foreign aid—to be weighted down with the political burden of extraneous controversial issues. Just as the aid program has been made a battleground for such irrelevancies as America's relations with Yugoslavia, Ecuadoran interference with American fishing vessels, and the mistreatment of Jews in the Soviet Union, education has been made a battleground for the most abrasive issues in our domestic policy.

I do not suggest that there is no connection between education on the one hand and problems relating to civil rights and parochial schools on the other. Indeed, there is a profound connection. But instead of building an intelligent and constructive relationship by bringing the healing powers of learning to bear on the agitated issues of religion and race, we have allowed the angry emotions aroused by these issues to defeat one effort after another to provide a better education for our children. In politics the surest way to accomplish nothing is by trying to accomplish everything. I for one am totally unable to understand how a Catholic child in a parochial school or a Negro child in a segregated school is benefited when the Federal Government fails to do anything for any school.

Largely because of the initiatives taken by Presidents Kennedy and Johnson, the sterile and obstinate insistence on tying education to problems of religion and race seems to be breaking down. A new and more constructive spirit is taking hold, in part, no doubt, because the adoption of the Civil Rights Act of 1964 has removed that issue, at least temporarily, from the arena of acute partisan controversy. We are beginning to understand—if I am not too optimistic—that problems of education and religion and race can best be dealt with each in their own terms and that, in addition, progress achieved in any one of these areas is quite likely to contribute to progress in the others. If this prognosis is correct, there are solid grounds for optimism as to the prospects for an effective national program of support for public education.

Optimism is certainly warranted by the words of President Johnson in his message on the state of the union and by the program for education which he submitted to the Congress on January 12. His recommendations for a program of assistance to needy and deserving students at all levels are a promising beginning in a vital and long-neglected field. It is to be hoped—and I daresay expected—that these recommendations will be translated into a large-scale and effective national program calculated to meet the educational needs of our youth. It is indeed a hopeful sign, and a tribute to the President's leadership, that his recommendations have thus far won the endorsement of both the National Education Association and the National Catholic Welfare Conference.

The President's education message is a work of high political creativity. Judging from the initial reaction, it appears to meet the two essential criteria of effective political action: it goes a long way toward resolving a national problem and it does so by means that are satisfactory or at least tolerable to all interested parties. By orienting the program to the pressing needs of children of low-income families, the President appears successfully to have bypassed the highly emotional issue of aid to parochial schools, which has hitherto defeated even the most concerted efforts to provide Federal assistance for education.

The President has undertaken not to resolve the constitutional question involved in aid to parochial schools but simply to separate it from the social and intellectual problem of strengthening education. Some may not admire the political artistry of this approach, but others—and I am among them—will share the view expressed by President Homer Babbidge of the University of Connecticut, who has said: "It is surely true that no society—in the world at least—has ever been able to afford the luxury of facing squarely all the issues that divide its people. The use of fiction as an instrument of cohesion is an indispensable social tool."

There is, in my mind, no question as to the need and desirability of Federal assistance to education. Education is a national problem which requires national solutions. Because of the mobility of our people and the interdependence of every element of our national economy, an inadequate school system in any one state adversely affects the entire nation. The Federal Government is uniquely qualified to raise the money needed to finance improvements in local school systems, and its obligation to do so derives from the fact that the entire nation suffers when any of our citizens are denied the best possible education.

As to the cost of a program of Federal aid to education, it will be considerable. Good education is not and cannot be cheap but I can think of no area of public policy in which we can expect greater returns for our money. Surely, in the long run, the education of our youth is as important to the security of our country as the maintenance of a powerful defense establishment and a good deal more important than a voyage to the moon. To those who shrink in the name of economy from a national commitment to education, I commend the words of Edmund Burke, that "economy is a distributive virtue, and consists not in saving but in selection. Parsimony requires no providence, no sagacity, no powers of combination, no comparison, no judgment."

In modern America, for the first time in human history, the opportunity has arisen to bring virtually an entire population into the quest for a higher order of happiness and fulfillment. This opportunity is the gift of a richly endowed continent and the advanced technology which has developed it. It is an opportunity of unprecedented promise and magnitude, but its realization depends upon the expenditure of enormous resources of knowledge and skill. The production of these human resources is the task of American education, which is thus confronted with an extraordinary challenge and opportunity.

The pursuit of human excellence is more than an opportunity; it is a necessity as well. It is a necessity if we are to retain control over the effects of modern technology, a necessity for coping with such potentially destructive problems as the worldwide population explosion, and a necessity for the introduction of some order and security in a world subject to the ever present threat of nuclear destruction.

The technology of an automated economy has created the need for an altogether new order of human resources. A high level of public education is no longer merely enriching for the individual and desirable for the society; it is becoming absolutely essential for the employment of the individual and for the economic growth and stability of the society. Specifically, our increasingly automated economy requires a highly educated elite to create and sustain the new technology and a highly skilled labor force to operate the complex machinery of the new technology. Meanwhile opportunities for unskilled labor are constantly diminishing. It is estimated that in the United States today something like $10,000 in what has been called "intellectual capital," that is to say, the cost of education, has been invested in each member of the labor force now employed. It is clear that for purposes of employment and economic growth a high degree of education has become essential not just for some of our people, but for the great majority of them.

The worldwide population explosion is another critical problem which is unlikely to be brought under control except through the application of advanced scientific knowledge by great numbers of people with at least enough basic education to understand the importance of the problem. The economically underdeveloped countries of the world are for the most part also the countries of highest population growth. Year by year these countries are seeing their painfully achieved gains in industry and food production wiped out, and more than wiped out, by uncontrolled population growth. On the basis of an estimate of the population of the world at the time of the birth of Christ, it took fifteen hundred years for the world's population to double. At present, the world's population is increasing by about fifty million a year. If this rate continues, the population of the world will double itself, from just under four billion to eight billion, in forty-five years.

With uncontrolled population growth already outrunning resources and destined, if not brought under control, to outrun them catastrophically, it is a matter of the greatest urgency for scientists to develop a cheap and simple method of birth control and—what is likely to be far more difficult—for governments and educators to bring hundreds of millions of poor and uneducated people to understand the necessity of population control.

The problem of population control is only to a very limited extent a technical one. There are technical difficulties, to be sure, but these have proven far more tractable than the political and educational problems. There is reason for hope, however, that in this field as in that of education the political stalemate is about to be broken and that it will soon be possible to take effective action to gain control of the growth of the world's population.

The progress achieved has been the result of public educational efforts and timely political initiatives. In December of 1963 I was able for the first time—and then only with some difficulty—to persuade my colleagues to accept an amendment to the foreign aid bill authorizing the use of limited funds to study the problem of population growth. An extremely important step forward was taken by President Johnson twelve days ago in his State of the Union message. "I will seek new ways," he said, "to use our knowledge to help deal with the explosion in world population and the growing scarcity of world resources." This, I believe, was the first time that an American President has given public and official sanction to efforts to deal with the uncontrolled growth of population.

It is to be hoped that educators in America and abroad will follow up the President's political initiative with programs for educating great numbers of people to the economic and demographic problems of unlimited population growth. The problem was generated in large part by advances in science, notably in medicine and food production, but as Lord Brain, the eminent British neurologist, has pointed out, the roots of scientific problems—and therefore their solution—are in society itself. "The scientist," he says, "is a member of society, and it is society which educates him, pays him for his work, and neglects to foresee its consequences. And society is responsible for what it does or fails to do with the scientist's discoveries." As applied to the problem of population control, the meaning of Lord Brain's observation is that the responsibility for action lies more with educators than with scientists.

Education has vital responsibilities both for advancing modern technology and for putting it to civilized and intelligent uses. Technology deals with the means of life not its ends. The ends of life have to do with the individual—with his dignity and character and happiness and freedom. The ends of human life have not been altered by profound changes in its means and conditions. Man's basic aims have remained the same, and so, therefore, has liberal education, which is concerned with man's nature and needs, with the uses of technology for the advancement of human welfare, and with the eternal effort to bring reason and justice and humanity into the relations of men and nations.

Education for these purposes is liberal education; it is literature and philosophy and history and the arts. Far from being less important in this age of advanced technology, these disciplines are more critically important than ever in the past, because they have to do with the most critically important question of our time, which is whether technology is going to be an instrument of human happiness or the vehicle of our destruction.

I share the belief that Professor Ruhl Bartlett expressed in these words:

I will not despair of the human race as long as our institutions of education continue to place the highest priority on the ends of life. When this ceases to be true, we will be in peril. For we will soon have a new slavery to the machine and the state, a new dark age of superstition and fear, and a new primitive order where the chief occupation of the human race is survival. I believe that all people who have had the opportunity and privilege of liberal education have a duty to see to it that this does not happen.

In no single area of human activity are the resources of liberal education of greater importance than in international relations, most particularly in relations between the great nations whose military technology has given them the power to destroy humanity without, so far as we know, endowing them with the wisdom to refrain from doing so. There is a gap—a very large gap—between technical power and human wisdom in international relations. The effort to close that gap must surely be considered one of the surpassing challenges to both statesmanship and scholarship.

Problems of East-West relations very often have to do with technology, but the problems themselves are not technological but political. The arms race, for example, is a competition in military technology, but neither its causes nor its consequences are primarily technological. Its primary consequence, in fact, has been a steady decrease in the military security of both great nuclear powers as each has acquired a growing arsenal of weapons with which to devastate the other. The cause of the arms race is political and psychological and so, if there is one, is the cure.

Our relations with the Soviet Union and other Communist countries require the application of the kinds of insight and understanding that only the most broadly based liberal education can provide. We must bring to our conduct of East-West relations some of the perspectives of history and philosophy and psychology. We must apply the experience of the past with intelligence and discrimination, separating those experiences which seem to have general application from those which were unique or accidental. We must recognize that history can be misleading as well as instructive, and we must avoid the pitfall of simple and literal analogy—such as the eternally repeated example of Munich, which is so often cited as an object lesson for cases which it resembles only slightly or superficially. We must utilize our knowledge of man and his past in the only way it can be utilized, not as a source of detailed prescriptions for specific maladies but as a source of general insight into the kinds of efforts that are likely to succeed and the kinds that are likely to fail, the kinds of policies that are likely to advance the cause of peace and the kinds that are likely not to. And, in addition, we must try to follow Aldous Huxley's advice "to look at the world directly and not through the half-opaque medium of concepts, which distorts every given fact into the all too familiar likeness of some generic label or explanatory abstraction."

More important than any single policy decision that we might make, or any change in the direction of our policy, is the strengthening of our capacity to reconsider established policies in the light of changing facts and circumstances. As President Kirk of Columbia recently pointed out, "The reconsideration of any policy does not necessarily lead to major changes; it could merely reaffirm the general conclusion that, despite new situations, the original policy and the basis upon which it was constructed remain as sound as ever." It is not change itself that is needed in our current relations with Communist countries but the *capacity* for change. I believe that most of our present policies toward the Communist countries are sound, but I am not at all confident that we would be prepared to alter these policies quickly in response to a wholly new situation or an unforeseen opportunity. The problem of our policy is thus more nearly intellectual than political. It is a problem of freeing our minds from the dead weight of habit and prejudice and stereotype and of bringing to bear on foreign policy the rich and diverse resources of liberally educated men.

The problems of public policy come back to the need for quality and creativity in all the diverse pursuits of our democratic society. Solutions to the entire range of our national problems—from automation to the world population explosion to dealing with the Communists—depend ultimately on whether we fill our personal and community lives with trivial occupations or with meaningful and intelligent occupations, on whether or not we maintain what Professor Perry has called "an express insistence upon quality and distinction."

In the past generation the emphasis of our public policy has been heavily weighted on measures for the common defense to the considerable neglect of programs for promoting the welfare and happiness of our people. The reason for this, of course, has been the exacting demands of two world wars and an intractable cold war, which have wrought vast changes in the character of American life.

Wealth and talent have been diverted on a massive scale from individual and community life to the increasingly complex and costly effort to maintain an adequate level of national security in a world in which no nation can be immune from the threat of sudden catastrophe. We have had to turn away from our hopes in order to concentrate on our fears and the result has been accumulating neglect of those things which bring happiness and beauty and fulfillment into our lives. The "public happiness," in August Heckscher's term, has become a luxury to be postponed to some distant day when the dangers that now beset us will have disappeared.

This, I think, is the real meaning of the cold war in American life. It has consumed money and time and talent that could otherwise be used to build schools and homes and hospitals, to remove the blight of ugliness that is spreading over the cities and highways of America, and to overcome the poverty and hopelessness that afflict the lives of one fifth of the people in an otherwise affluent society. It has put a high premium on avoiding innovation at home because new programs involve controversy as well as expense and it has been felt that we could not afford domestic divisions at a time when external challenges required us to maintain the highest possible degree of national unity. Far more pervasively than the United Nations or the "Atlantic community" could ever do, the cold war has encroached upon our sovereignty; it has given the Communists the major voice in determining what proportion of our Federal budget must be allocated to the military and what proportion, therefore, cannot be made available for domestic social and economic projects. This is the price that we have been paying for the cold war and it has been a high price indeed.

The cold war, it seems clear, has been an excuse as well as a genuine cause for the diversion of our energies from domestic well-being to external security. We have been preoccupied with foreign affairs for twenty-five years, and while striking progress has been made in certain areas of our national life, the agenda of neglect has grown steadily longer. We can no longer afford to defer problems of slums and crime and poverty and inadequate education until some more tranquil time in the future. These problems have become urgent if not intolerable in an affluent society. It is entirely reasonable to defer domestic programs in time of an all-out national effort such as World War II, but in the present cold war it is not reasonable to defer our domestic needs until more tranquil times, for the simple reason that there may be no more tranquil times in this generation or in this century.

In the long run, the solution of our domestic problems has as vital a bearing on the success of our foreign policies as on the public happiness at home. We must therefore reassess the priorities of our public policy, with a view to redressing the disproportion between our military and space efforts on the one hand and our education and human welfare programs on the other. We must distinguish between necessity and preference in our preoccupation with national security, judging our military needs by a standard which takes due account of the fact that armaments are only one aspect of national security, that military power, as one observer [Kenneth W. Thompson] has written, "is like the fist whose force depends on the health and vitality of the body politic and the whole society."

There are good reasons for believing that the American people and their leaders have become actively aware of the vital relationship between foreign and domestic policy and of the great importance of closing the gap between our production and consumption of human resources. There are strong indications that the Congress and the American people as well as the President are prepared to launch new and creative programs in various areas of our domestic life, especially education. These programs are as important for our foreign relations as for our domestic affairs because the challenge of all public policy is at bottom one of quality and creativity in our national life.

It is a challenge that ultimately falls back on our educational institutions. To a certain degree a United States Senator can point the way toward intelligent and creative policies as he sees them; to a much greater degree the President of the United States can do so; but the ultimate answer to the challenge of excellence lies with public school teachers and university professors, with writers and scholars and all those who in one way or another help to shape the minds, or fail to shape the minds, of young Americans. "A teacher affects eternity," wrote Henry Adams; "he can never tell where his influence stops."

APPENDIX

BIOGRAPHICAL NOTES

ACHESON, DEAN (1893-). Born, Middletown, Connecticut; A.B., Yale University, 1915; M.A. (honorary), 1936; LL.B., Harvard University, 1918; LL.D., Wesleyan University, 1947; Yale University, 1962; D.C.L., Oxford University, 1952; Cambridge University, 1958; and other honorary degrees; secretary to Louis Brandeis, 1919-21; with law firm of Covington, Burling and Rublee, Washington, D.C., 1921-33; Covington, Burling, Rublee, Acheson and Shorb, 1934-41; Covington and Burling, 1953- ; Assistant Secretary of State, 1941-45; Under Secretary of State, 1945-47; Secretary of State, 1949-53; Order of Vasa (Sweden), Aztec Eagle, and other awards; author, *A Democrat Looks at His Party,* 1955; *A Citizen Looks at Congress,* 1957; *Power and Diplomacy,* 1958. (See also *Current Biography: 1949.*)

FULBRIGHT, JAMES WILLIAM (1905-). Born, Sumner, Missouri; A.B., University of Arkansas, 1925; B.A., Oxford University, 1928; M.A.; 1931; LL.B. with distinction, George Washington University, 1934; many honorary degrees; admitted to District of Columbia bar, 1934; special attorney, Antitrust Division, Department of Justice, 1934-35; instructor in law, George Washington University, 1935-36; lecturer in law, University of Arkansas, 1936-39; president, University of Arkansas, 1939-41; United States House of Representatives (Democrat, Arkansas), 1943-45; United States Senate, 1945- ; chairman, United States delegation to London Conference of Allied Ministers of Education, 1944; instrumental in establishing program for American scholars to study abroad; chairman, Foreign Relations Committee, United States Senate; Rhodes scholar; Phi Beta Kappa; author, *Old Myths and New Realities, and Other Commentaries,* 1964. (See also *Current Biography: 1955.*)

GOHEEN, ROBERT FRANCIS (1919-). Born, Vengurla, India; A.B., Princeton University, 1940; M.A., 1947; Ph.D., 1948; LL.D., University of Madras, 1957; Harvard University, 1957; Yale University, 1957; Litt. D., Brown University, 1958; L.H.D., St. Mary's College, 1963; and other honorary degrees; teacher of classics, Princeton University, 1945-57; president, 1957- ; senior fellow in classics, American Academy in Rome, 1952-53; director, national Woodrow Wilson fellowship program, 1953-56; director, American Council on Education; member of board, Woodrow Wilson Foundation; Carnegie Foundation for the Advancement of Teaching; in military service, 1941-45; recipient, Bronze Star; author, *The Image of Sophocles' Antigone,* 1951. (See also *Current Biography: 1958.*)

GOLDWATER, BARRY MORRIS (1909-). Born, Phoenix, Arizona; student, Staunton Military Academy and University of Arizona, 1928; associated with Goldwater's Inc. since 1929; president, 1937-53; councilman, Phoenix, 1949-52; United States Senate (Republican, Arizona), 1953-64; Republican candidate for President of the United States, 1964; member, Armed Services Commission; member, advisory Commission on Indian Affairs, Department of the Interior, 1948-50; pilot, United States Army Air Force, 1941-45; major general, United States Air Force Reserves; man of year, Phoenix, 1949; author, *Arizona Portraits,* 1940; *Journey Down the River of Canyons,* 1940; *Speeches of Henry Ashurst,* 1960; *The Conscience of a Conservative,* 1960; *Why Not Victory?* 1962; *Let's Try Freedom.* (See also *Current Biography: 1955.*)

JOHNSON, LYNDON BAINES (1908-). Born near Stonewall, Texas; graduate, Johnson City (Texas) high school, 1924; B.S., Southwest State Teachers College, San Marcos, 1930; student, Georgetown University Law School, 1935-36; teacher, public schools, Houston, Texas, 1930-32; secretary to Representative Richard M. Kleberg, 1932-35; state director, National Youth Administration for Texas, 1935-37; member, United States House of

Representatives (Democrat, Texas), 1937-49; United States Senate, 1949-61; minority leader, 83rd Congress; majority leader, 84th-86th Congresses; resigned from United States Senate, January 3, 1961; Vice President of the United States, 1961-63; became President of the United States upon the assassination of President Kennedy, November 22, 1963; elected President of the United States, 1964; author, *My Hope for America*, 1964. (See also *Current Biography: 1964.*)

McGEE, GALE (1915-). Born, Lincoln, Nebraska; A.B., Nebraska State Teachers College (Wayne), 1936; active in debate and oratory; A.M., University of Colorado, 1939; Ph.D., University of Chicago, 1947; teacher of history and speech, Crafton, Nebraska, high school, 1936-37; Kearney, Nebraska, high school, 1937-40; assistant professor of speech and debate and history, Nebraska Wesleyan University, 1940-43; instructor, American history, Iowa State College, 1943-44; Notre Dame, 1944-45; assistant instructor, University of Chicago, 1945-46; professor of history, University of Wyoming, 1946-58; United States Senate (Democrat, Wyoming), 1958- . (See also *Current Biography: 1961.*)

MILLER, SAMUEL H. (1900-). Born, Philadelphia, Pennsylvania; student, Massachusetts Institute of Technology, 1917-18; B.Th., Colgate University, 1923; D.D., 1953; Litt. D., Clark University, 1959; ordained, Baptist ministry, 1923; minister, Calvary Baptist Church, Belmar, New Jersey, 1923-28; Arlington, New Jersey, 1928-30; First Baptist Church, Clifton, New Jersey, 1930-35; Old Cambridge Church, Cambridge, Massachusetts, 1935-59; lecturer, Harvard Divinity School, 1954-58; professor of pastoral theology, 1958-59; dean, 1959- ; author, *The Life of the Soul*, 1951; *The Life of the Church*, 1953; *Great Realities*, 1955; *Prayers for Daily Use*, 1957.

MORSE, WAYNE (1900-). Born, Madison, Wisconsin; Ph.B., University of Wisconsin, 1923; A.M., 1924; LL.B., University of

Minnesota, 1928; J.D., Columbia University, 1932; other honorary degrees; instructor, University of Wisconsin, 1924; assistant professor of argumentation, University of Minnesota, 1924-28; teaching fellow, Columbia University, 1928-29; assistant professor of law, University of Oregon, 1929-30; associate professor, 1930-31; deàn of law school, 1931-44; special assistant to United States Attorney General, 1936-39; Pacific coast arbitrator, United States Department of Labor, 1938-42; member, National War Labor Board, 1942-44; United States Senate (Oregon), 1945- (Republican, 1945-52; Independent, 1952-55; Democrat, 1955-); author, *A Survey of the Grand Jury System*, 1931; co-author, *The Administration of Criminal Justice in Oregon*, 1932. (See also *Current Biography: 1954*.)

RUSK, DEAN (1909-). Born, Cherokee County, Georgia; A.B., Davidson College, 1931; B.S., St. John's College, Oxford University, 1933; M.A., 1934; LL.D., Mills College, 1948; Davidson College, 1950; Princeton University, 1961; and other honorary degrees; associate professor of government and dean, Mills College, 1934-40; assistant chief, Division of International Security Affairs, United States Department of State, 1946; Special Assistant Secretary of War, 1946-47; director, office of United Nations affairs, Department of State, 1947-49; Assistant Secretary of State, February 1949; Deputy Under Secretary of State, 1949-50; Assistant Secretary of State for Far Eastern Affairs, 1950-51; president, Rockefeller Foundation, 1952-60; Secretary of State, 1961- ; Legion of Merit. (See also *Current Biography: 1961*.)

SEABORG, GLENN T. (1912-). Born, Ishpeming, Michigan; A.B., University of California at Los Angeles, 1934; Ph.D., University of California at Berkeley, 1937; instructor in chemistry, University of California at Berkeley, 1939-41; assistant professor, 1941; professor, 1945; announced discovery of plutonium (atomic number 94), 1940; associated with Manhattan Project on creation of atomic bomb, 1942-46; returned to teaching, 1946; associate director, Lawrence Radiation Laboratory, 1954-58; member of advisory committee to Atomic Energy Commission, 1946-50; shared Nobel Prize in chemistry with E. M. McMillan for work on transuranium elements, 1951; Fermi Award, 1959; member of President Eisenhower's science advisory committee, 1959; chancellor, University of California at Berkeley, 1958-61; chairman, Atomic Energy Commission, 1961- ; frequent contributor to scientific journals; co-author, *Comprehensive Inorganic Chemistry I*, 1953; *The Chemistry of the Actinide Elements*, 1957; *Elements of the Universe*, 1958. (See also *Current Biography: 1961*.)

STEVENSON, ADLAI E. (1900-1965). Born, Los Angeles, California; attended public schools in Bloomington, Illinois, high school of Illinois State Normal University, and Choate School; A.B., Princeton University, 1922; LL.D., 1954; J.D., Northwestern University, 1926; LL.D., 1949; many other honorary degrees; admitted to Illinois bar, 1926; practiced in Chicago, 1927-33; partner in law firm, 1935-41; assistant to Secretary of Navy, 1941-44; chief, economic mission to Italy, 1943; assistant to Secretary of State, 1945; adviser, United States delegation, Conference on International Organization in San Francisco, 1945; chief, United States delegation, Preparatory Commission of the United Nations, London, 1945; United States delegate to General Assembly, 1946, 1947; governor of Illinois, 1949-53; Democratic candidate for President of the United States, 1952, 1956; with law firm, Chicago, 1955, 1957-60; United States Representative to the United Nations, 1960-65; died, London, July 14, 1965; Distinguished Service Award, United States Navy, 1956; author, *Call to Greatness*, 1954; *What I Think*, 1956; *The New America*, 1957; *Friends and Enemies: What I Learned in Russia*, 1958; *Putting First Things First*, 1960; *Looking Outward: Years of Crisis at the United Nations*, 1963. (See also *Current Biography: 1961*.)

TAYLOR, WILLIAM L. (1931-). Born, Brooklyn, New York; B.A. (cum laude), Brooklyn College, 1952; LL.B., Yale Law School, 1954; staff attorney, NAACP legal defense and educational fund, 1954-58; legislative representative, Americans for

Democratic Action, 1959-61; special assistant to staff director, United States Commission on Civil Rights, May 1961-May 1962; assistant staff director for liaison and information, May 1962-October 1963; general counsel, 1963- ; staff director designate, 1965; United States Army, 1956-58; contributor to legal publications.

TRUEBLOOD, D. ELTON (1900-). Born, Pleasantville, Iowa; A.B., William Penn College, 1922; active in debating and extemporaneous speaking; B.S.T., Harvard School of Theology, 1926; Ph.D., Johns Hopkins University, 1934; assistant professor of philosophy and dean of men, Guilford College, 1927-30; assistant professor of philosophy, Haverford College, 1933-36; chaplain and professor of philosophy, Stanford University, 1936-45; professor of philosophy, Earlham College, 1946- ; founder, Earlham School of Religion, 1963; president, Yokefellow Associates; editor, *The Friend*, 1935-47; recipient, Churchman of the Year Award, Religious Heritage of America, 1960; author of many books including *Foundations for Reconstruction*, 1946; *Philosophy of Religion*, 1957; *The Yoke of Christ*, 1958; *The Idea of College*, 1959; *Confronting Christ*, 1960; *The Company of the Committed*, 1961; *The Humor of Christ*, 1964. (See also *Current Biography: 1964*.)

WERT, ROBERT JOSEPH (1922-). Born, Harrison, Idaho; A.B., Stanford University, 1943; M.B.A., 1950; Ph.D., 1952; student at Harvard Graduate School of Business Administration, 1944; secretary-treasurer, Long Lake Lumber Company of Spokane, 1946-49; assistant to president, Stanford University, 1951-54; vice provost and dean of undergraduate education, 1959- ; executive associate, Carnegie Corporation, 1954-59; president, California Coordinating Council on Higher Education, 1960- ; member, California Master Plan Survey Team, 1959-60; United States Naval Reserve, 1943-46.

WHITNEY, JOHN HAY (1904-). Born, Ellsworth, Maine; Groton School, 1916-22; Yale University, 1922-26; Oxford University, 1926-27; L.H.D., Kenyon College, 1958; M.A. (honorary), Yale University, 1959; LL.D., Colby College, 1964; other honorary degrees; United States ambassador to Great Britain, 1956-61; publisher, New York *Herald Tribune,* 1957-61; editor in chief and publisher, 1961- ; president, John Hay Whitney Foundation; member, Commission on Foreign Economic Policy, 1954; trustee, Museum of Modern Art; Carnegie Endowment for International Peace; colonel, United States Air Force, World War II; recipient, Yale Medal, 1954; Legion of Merit; associated with English Speaking Union.

CUMULATIVE AUTHOR INDEX

1960-1961—1964-1965

A cumulative author index to the volumes of REPRESENTATIVE AMERICAN SPEECHES for the years 1937-1938 through 1959-1960 appears in the 1959-1960 volume.